Flavor for *Mixed* Media

A *feast* OF TECHNIQUES FOR TEXTURE, COLOR AND LAYERS

Mary Beth Shaw

NORTH LIGHT BOOKS
Cincinnati, Ohio

15 14 13 12 11   5 4 3 2 1

Distributed in Canada by Fraser Direct
100 Armstrong Avenue
Georgetown, ON, Canada L7G 5S4
Tel: (905) 877-4411

Distributed in the U.K. and Europe by F+W Media International
Brunel House, Newton Abbot, Devon, TQ12 4PU, England
Tel: (+44) 1626 323200, Fax: (+44) 1626 323319
Email: postmaster@davidandcharles.co.uk
Distributed in Australia by Capricorn Link
P.O. Box 704, S. Windsor, NSW 2756 Australia
Tel: (02) 4577-3555

Library of Congress Cataloging-in-Publication Data

Shaw, Mary Beth.
  Flavor for mixed media / Mary Beth Shaw.
      p. cm.
  Includes bibliographical references and index.
  ISBN-13: 978-1-4403-0317-3 (pbk. : alk. paper)
  ISBN-10: 1-4403-0317-7 (pbk. : alk. paper)
  1. Mixed media painting--Technique. I. Title.
  ND1505.S48 2011
  702.8'1--dc22
                                    2010027696

www.fwmedia.com

Editor Tonia Davenport
Designer Ronson Slagle
Cover Designer Geoff Raker
Production Coordinator Greg Nock
Photographer Christine Polomsky

DEDICATION

This book is dedicated to my husband John; he is my rock and my foundation. Thank you for supporting me unconditionally and being such a patient (and smart!) sounding board. I love you.

Acknowledgments

Thank you to my parents and my family and friends, far and near. I am truly blessed. To my grandsons, Aidan and Ian, thank you for keeping me in the moment—what a gift; there is nothing better than having you (and my critters) in the studio with me.

Tonia, you are simply the best, and I don't know how I got so lucky. Thank you so very much—you and everyone at North Light—for giving me this amazing chance to live my dream (and for also making me look so good). A special thank you to my amazing guest artists—I am surrounded by brilliance at every turn!

And to all those who have moved on: Nathan, Michael, Gam and my grandparents. I miss you all so much. I hope you break open the champagne and give each other a big ol' high five. "I am not going to die, I'm going home like a shooting star."—Sojourner Truth

Contents

Art: A Feast for the Senses ...7

Preparation 8

Color 13

Guest Artist: Misty Mawn 14

Painting Without Paint 16

Guest Artist: Sarah Ahearn Bellemare 22

Triad Color Theory 24

Guest Artist: Elizabeth MacCrellish............... 28

Organic Abstract Painting............................. 30

Texture 35

Guest Artist: Shari Beaubien....................... 36

Clayboard Book 38

Guest Artist: Susan Tuttle 42

Texture Sampler.. 44

Guest Artist: Laura Lein-Svencner 46

Candle Shade 48

Layers..................................57

Guest Artist: Julie Snidle............................. 58

Collagraph Plate 60

Guest Artist: Tonia Davenport 64

Plexi Squared 66

Guest Artist: Dolan Geiman........................ 72

Three-Dimensional Painting........................... 74

Flavors...........................79

Guest Artist: Heather Haymart 80

Icing Panels.................................82

Guest Artist: Deb Trotter 86

Taste of Klimt................................88

Guest Artist: Claudine Hellmuth 94

Collage Painting.............................96

Combinations....................101

Guest Artist: Katie Kendrick 102

Cardboard Collage 104

Guest Artist: John Hammons......................108

Abstract Letter Forms 110

Guest Artist: Judy Wise 114

Abstract With Discarded Material...............116

Gallery..............................120

Guest Artists......................124

Resources 125

Index 126

About Mary Beth 127

Art: A *feast* for the Senses

Art and food: Two of life's most sensory pleasures and certainly two of my favorite things. I love it when I see a painting so alive with texture and color that I dash home to grab my paintbrush, or when I eat food that makes me moan out loud. Have you ever done that? Being the way I am—an artist who is also a foodie—I have pondered the similarities between art and food and am utterly convinced the processes of creating art and cooking are very much the same.

Art and food are the stuff of memories. Think back to your childhood. So many celebrations and family outings involved food. I remember my mom's brown butter noodles; a dish she made frequently until the time my brother gorged himself sick, thus ending our noodle love affair. Then there were my Grandma's homemade doughnuts. I would lurk in her kitchen, allegedly helping, but really just trying to sneak a hunk of dough, which I shaped in my hands and dipped into sugar before eating—raw, of course.

As for art, I fondly remember Saturday morning drives to the Cincinnati Art Museum where I took classes as a child. I will never forget the huge piece of paper I was given. It was probably just newsprint or some such thing, but it seemed so important as we sprawled on the floor of the museum. And, incredibly, my parents still display the larger-than-life Kool-Aid packet (it was the '70s, what can I say?) I made in the eighth grade.

So imagine you get to attend a potluck dinner along with some of your favorite artists. Imagine they each bring a fabulous mixed-media piece. Everyone is lounging around the table, noshing on food, imbibing beverages, sharing their stories and talking about art.

That's what we're going to do. We're headed on an artistic culinary journey.

I will show you how to make art that is simple yet sumptuous, complex yet accessible and always filled with passion. You will learn how to make art that fuels your heart and soul. No matter your experience level, you are sure to relish this artsy sojourn.

For me, with art or with food, I generally start out with a recipe or an idea and then somewhere along the way deviate into another direction. I am providing you with both techniques and projects. The book is divided into sections: Color, Texture, Layers, Flavors and Combinations. You can read straight through or skip around however you wish.

Throughout the book, you will see sidebars titled *What's in Your Pantry?* These are designed to offer options regarding substitutions and variations for the projects. Much like cooking, mixed media offers ample opportunity to experiment, and I find that I often get my best results when I deviate from the so-called "recipe."

You will be treated to flavorful eye candy as we look at the treats our guest artists share. Each of them has inspired me to explore spicy new mixed-media techniques as well as fresh twists on old techniques. You'll hear stories about art and food and eating and creating. I will share lots of recipes for creating interesting art and even recipes for actual foodstuffs. When it's all said and done, we can raise our glasses to the glorious diversity we fondly call mixed media.

PREPARATION

Just like stocking a pantry, furnishing your art room or studio requires preparation. When I was first getting serious about my art, I bought every supply I could get my hands on—the more, the merrier. Or so I thought. Then I got kinda over- whelmed. I spent a lot of time playing with each and every supply to figure out what did what and the variety of effects I could achieve. It was trial by error, and I made ugly messes. These days I try to minimize my supplies slightly, but oh I can't help myself. I still adore trying new things.

So, as you can imagine, I have tons of media in my studio. I think of all my sup- plies, media and substrates like a giant spice rack. In other words, I don't necessarily use every single item every single time. I tend to pick and choose judiciously as I work through an individual piece.

Luck is what happens when preparation meets opportunity.
—Seneca

Substrates

Before starting a project, I generally consider which substrate will serve my need best. I enjoy working on a variety of surfaces because I think it's a good way to stay fresh. Each substrate responds differently, and I switch back and forth to exploit their differences and keep my work loose.

For the last few years, claybord (I generally use Ampersand Claybord) has been an ongoing fave of mine. The smooth, slick surface is challenging yet forgiving and has traits that simply cannot be found in other surfaces. Paper is my good old reliable, and I always have a stash of watercolor paper in the studio, typically 140 lb. (300gsm) or above in a variety of sizes. I prefer smooth hot-pressed paper, but sometimes will grab cold press just to do something different. I also keep lots and lots of canvas panels for small projects and stretched canvasses—most of them gallery wrapped. Lately I have enjoyed working on panels and boards—MDF, Masonite, that sort of thing. You can buy these boards at art stores or go to the hardware store and then cut them yourself. During the course of this book, we will explore each surface in depth so you can learn the differences.

Color

For color, I mix it up to the max by using a lot of different products to create color effects—pastels (soft and oil), acrylic paints, markers and inks. For soft pastels (like chalk), I am partial to super soft ones—Sennelier or Unison. (Be safe when using dusty pastels and wear a mask to protect yourself from airborne particles.) I also use PanPastels. Oil pastels are fun to "pop" color at the end of the project. Because they are waxy and it is difficult to layer over them, I limit their usage to the final stages of a project. With respect to paints, I use both fluid and heavy body acrylics depending on the look desired. I am not loyal to a particular brand; I love paint so much how could I possibly limit myself? And acrylic markers are my new best friend—particularly the ones by Marvy—DecoColor Acrylic Paint Markers. I prefer them because they have a great range of colors and they don't have any of that stinky xylene.

And I adore inks! Acrylic, alcohol, airbrush, calligraphy . . . the runnier, the better. When you are buying inks, I caution you to know how they will react with the other media you are using. Unless the ink is waterproof, it will run if activated with water, even after it is dry. That may or may not be the effect you desire, so just be aware.

Organize the Pantry

Organization is key. If you have too much stuff and it's all over the place, the clutter will infiltrate your brain and impede your process. So take a minute (or two or three) and get organized. You will feel so much better.

For collage parts, I prefer clear storage so I can see what I've got. I organize by category when I have enough of a particular item, then by shape if I don't. For instance, numbers and letters are in one box, 3-D toys and doodads in another and stamps (Top Value, S+H) in yet another. Then miscellaneous round stuff is in its own bin, all linear stuff in another. I have a long chain (yep, just a hunk of chain) that hangs with gallon plastic bags hanging off S-hooks. One each of computer keys, puzzle pieces, beach glass, safety glass, copper parts . . . you get the idea. Easy to see and grab, easy to put away.

For art supplies, buckets work for pencils, markers, tube paint. I have different parts of the studio set up for different functions, and the things I use in each area are within an arm's reach.

Figure out what works for you, and don't be afraid to change if your first round of organization doesn't work out. It took me years to get where I am now, and I still feel like it's a moving target.

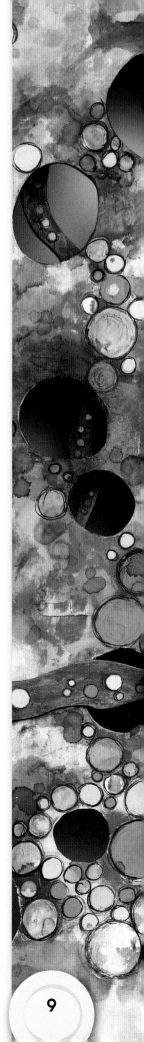

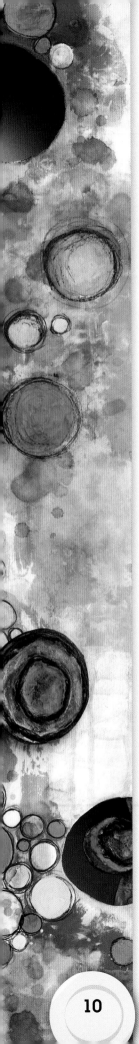

Glue

For gluing paper stuff, I use regular acrylic gel medium—always the glossy because it dries totally clear. I also use heavier glues as necessary and will mention those as we move forward. Generally I try to stick with stuff that is nontoxic, and I simply read the package to see what product will work best depending on the specific situation.

Collage

When I first started making collages, I became the dumping ground for everyone I knew, and I instantly assembled an enormous collection of all kinds of paper goods. In addition to this, I am a world-class scavenger and collect lots of stuff on my own: found stuff, discarded stuff, vintage, torn and burned stuff—yum, yum, yum. Most of my stash is paper, but I keep a steady supply of 3-D elements too. My family calls me out on this. Once, when with my stepdaughter, I picked up a smooshed metal sumpthin' (off the ground). She stopped in her tracks, looked at me and said, "Did you just pick up a piece of garbage?" Ahem. Needless to say, I also save all of my own so-called discards, even paper towels, because you never know when you can repurpose them.

Tools

Scissors and craft knives are integral to any collage artist. In addition, I use a variety of carving tools plus a Dremel rotary tool with various attachments. And sandpaper is my friend, lots and lots of those sanding blocks.

Food for Thought

I sometimes jokingly describe mixed media as "art for someone who can't make up their mind," which definitely describes me. I mean, who doesn't love paints and pens and inks and markers? You walk into the store, and there they are in all their lovely glory, lined up by color, just begging to come home with you. It is sometimes hard to know what will work with what. I go by a couple simple guidelines.

1. How do you clean it? If you can clean it up with water, it stands to reason it must be water-based, and all the water-based stuff works together—acrylic, watercolors and some inks. It is only when you mix water-based and oil-based media that you get into trouble. Then you simply need to remember the phrase "Fat over lean," which means you use acrylic and other water-based stuff first (lean) and put oil paint (or any other oil-based media) on last—or on top (fat).

2. The second thing I consider is whether the product is water-soluble or waterproof. I am mainly interested in this with respect to pens, pencils and markers. I want to know whether it will stay put or not. Fluid acrylic is very wet and will turn water-soluble marks into runny messes. I'm not saying I won't buy one or another, I just prefer to know this in advance.

These are my absolute favorite cookies
of all time. I make them a little on the thick side, and everyone in my family fights over the thickest cookies. I usually decorate them with icing.

Recipe for: Watkins Vanilla Sugar Cookies

from *The All American Cookie Book* by Nancy Baggett

- 2½ cups all-purpose white flour, sifted after measuring
- 1 tsp. baking powder
- 1 cup (2 sticks) unsalted butter, slightly softened
- 1 cup sugar
- 2 large egg yolks
- generous pinch of salt
- 2 tsp. vanilla extract
- 2–3 T. sugar for topping.

→ In a large bowl, thoroughly stir together the flour and baking powder; set aside. In another large bowl, with an electric mixer on medium speed, beat together the butter and sugar until well blended and fluffy. Beat in the egg yolks, then the salt and vanilla, until evenly incorporated. Gradually beat or stir in the flour mixture to form a smooth dough.

→ Divide the dough in half. Place each portion between large sheets of wax paper. Roll out each portion ⅛ inch thick; check the underside of the dough and smooth out any wrinkles that form. Stack the rolled portions (paper still attached) on a baking sheet. Refrigerate for about 30 minutes, or until cold and firm, or freeze for about 15 minutes to speed chilling.

→ Preheat the oven to 375°F (191°C). Grease several baking sheets or coat with nonstick spray.

→ Working with one portion at a time and leaving the remaining dough chilled, gently peel away, then pat one sheet of wax paper back into place. Flip the dough over, then peel off and discard the second sheet. Using assorted 2½- to 3-inch cutters, cut out the cookies. (If at any point the dough softens too much to handle easily, transfer the paper and cookies to a baking sheet and refrigerate or freeze until firm again.) Using a spatula, carefully transfer the cookies to the baking sheets, spacing about 1¼ inches apart. Reroll any dough scraps. Continue cutting out the cookies until all the dough is used. Sprinkle the cookies with the sugar.

→ Bake the cookies, one sheet at a time, in the upper third of the oven for 8 to 11 minutes, or until lightly colored on top and slightly darker at the edges. Reverse the sheet from front to back halfway through baking to ensure even browning. Transfer the sheet to a wire rack and let stand until the cookies firm up slightly, 1 to 2 minutes. Using a spatula, transfer the cookies to wire racks. Let stand until completely cooled.

→ Store in an airtight container for up to 2 weeks or freeze for up to 1 month.

COLOR

To whet your appetite, our "first course" is all about color. Color makes my heart sing, and when my heart sings, my work sings. And when my work sings, well, it makes me wanna dance. In addition to creating mood, color helps us to instill meaning into our work. Successful use of color will not only trigger emotional associations but can create nuance and personal references for each viewer.

In this, our first chapter, we welcome guest artists Misty Mawn, Sarah Ahearn Bellemare and Elizabeth MacCrellish, who will join us as we play with color. Their work inspires us to look at color from different vantage points. The projects in this chapter will explore a variety of ways to create and layer color with pastels, acrylics, airbrush paints and inks. We will drip and fling and splash and spray. We'll explore Painting Without Paint (huh!?) on clayboard. We'll review Triad Color Theory by trying a method that is so easy-peasy you won't believe it. And finally, we'll create an Organic Abstract Painting.

I see skies of blue, clouds of white, bright blessed days, dark sacred nights. And I think to myself, "What a wonderful world."
— Louis Armstrong

Guest Artist:
Misty Mawn

It sounds like a cliché to say that I think of the movie *Play Misty for Me* whenever I think about Misty Mawn, but I have to admit it's kind of true. Perhaps it has something to do with the fact that I spent time in northern California (where *Play Misty for Me* was filmed), and Misty's evocative work stirs memories for me. Her palette is reminiscent of the area, so incredibly beautiful yet with a foggy, or well, misty overtone that makes me want to curl up with a cushy blanket.

Misty Mawn has been making art all her life. As a teen, she remembers creating mix tapes for friends where she cut up things to make collages for the covers. On each one, she got more and more elaborate as she tried to outdo her previous effort. She went on to art school, where she studied studio art. After she got married, she started a pottery business, which put her out on the art fair scene for about seven years.

After tiring of pottery and art fairs, she eventually shut down the business and sadly, only kept a few plates as memories of that time. It was then she started to explore collage anew. She started selling on eBay, became recognized and was subsequently asked to write articles for magazines. She then got involved in the teaching circuit where she has been a popular draw, selling out classes left and right. The transition from 3-D to 2-D—something that could have been difficult—felt natural to her since she admits to having always struggled with making her three-dimensional pottery work convey the emotion that was in her head.

Anyone who has seen Misty's work will surely agree it is full of emotion and that she is a natural. The delicacy of the work, combined with its depth of passion, make it very compelling. Although I enjoy all her paintings, I am especially drawn to her monochromatic white pieces. She told me she likes the way the whites fall together with vintage appeal, leaving a slightly faded effect. For me, I feel as though I am viewing the pieces through the loveliest veil of silk.

As an avid cook, Misty agrees there is a definite similarity in the process of cooking and art making. Her cooking process starts with gathering, which is also her first step in making a collage. And although she is often inspired by a recipe, she has trouble following it and tends to make lots of changes. Changes that, I have no doubt, vastly improve the flavor.

Misty's Favorite Sandwich
Recipe for: *The Veggie Reuben*

- 1 clove garlic
- 2 raw carrots, diced
- 1 can chickpeas
- 1 can sauerkraut
- 1 bottle either Russian, French or Thousand Island dressing
- 6 slices of Havarti or provolone cheese
- 12 slices of really good rye bread

→ Preheat oven to 400°F (204°C).

→ In a food processor, blend garlic, chickpeas, carrots and ¼ cup dressing until thick and well blended. Butter one side of the rye bread and place that side down on a baking sheet. Layer the bread with a good helping of the chickpea mix. Next add a layer of sauerkraut, some dressing and a slice of cheese. Top with another piece of buttered bread (butter side up) and put it in the oven. Cook until toasted and the cheese has melted.

Painting Without Paint

One of my favorite things about Misty's work is her approach to color. I adore the limited palette and subtle hues she achieves in her white-on-white work. Inspired by her gorgeous painting, this project works with analogous colors in a most unusual way, without even touching paint.

Sounds crazy, right? Painting without paint? Laugh if you want, but I think you'll come to love this nontraditional process because it is much more forgiving than "real" painting. In fact, this is how I made most of my work before I became adept at mixing and managing paints. This project is reminiscent of a coloring book; it allows you to carve lines and then color in the spaces. The flexibility enables you to build lots of layers, but you can also go back and remove certain areas due to the unusual qualities inherent to clayboard. Let's get started so you can see what I'm talking about.

Ingredients

- pencil
- clayboard, smooth, flat panels, any size
- dental tools or any other hand-carving tools, such as ones manufactured by Ampersand
- cheese grater from dollar store
- soft pastels, a few monochromatic colors
- wire brush
- gesso
- paintbrushes
- acrylic matte medium
- airbrush paints
- spray bottle of water
- hair dryer
- oil pastels
- PanPastels
- acrylic paint markers (DecoArt)

1 Using a pencil, sketch out a rough composition on the clayboard.

2 Pick a few areas and carve out some texture using one of any number of tools. Dental tools work really well.

3 A handheld cheese grater makes wonderful texture. I place the clayboard on the edge of the table and hack at it with the grater, but do whatever works best for you.

4 Wire brushes come in a number of sizes and give you an interesting multiline texture. Experiment with tools and see what you like the best.

5 When you have completed creating texture, you are ready to begin adding the first layer of color using soft pastels. Pick several colors and color different areas of your piece. Note: Storing your pastels in rice flour will prevent colors from mixing with one another.

6 Put some gesso on your brush and work it into the pastels on the board. This is done with dabbing, stroking or scrubbing motions—try all three to see the difference in effect. Rinse your brush between colors. The gesso will blend and lighten the pastel. It will also fix the pastel into place on the clayboard so it is no longer airborne.

7 Alternatively, you can use matte medium instead of gesso to fix the pastel without changing its color. Work matte medium gently over the areas where you want the color more intense. Keep in mind that you don't need to create opaque blocks of color; the piece will actually be more interesting if there are value changes within each section. If you want the carved texture to show, be sure to work pastel into the recessed areas.

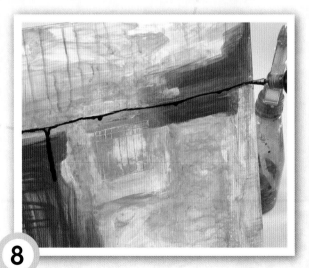

8 Using a contrasting color of airbrush paint, apply a line of color to the board, squeezing it directly from a bottle that has a tip on it.

9 Holding the board upright, spritz it with water to make the paint run.

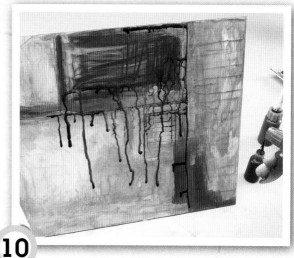

10 I like to turn the board once or twice to change the direction of the running paint.

11 Spritz again to make the ink drip more if desired. The more water you add, the more it will lighten the color of the ink.

12 A hair dryer can be used to alter or slow down the flow of the paint.

Painted Paper Towels

I always always always keep a damp paper towel in my hand, especially when I am spritzing water and creating drips. You never know when you might want to dab here or there and pull back some color. Sometimes after spraying, I use just the very corner of the paper towel to absorb ink from an isolated area. I buy solid white paper towels and use the same one over and over, laying it out to dry at the end of each day. They are very pretty and quite useful in other projects.

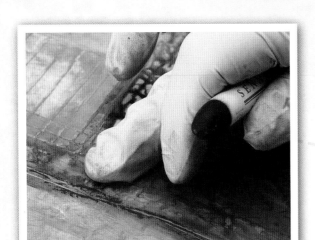

13

After the piece is dry, add more depth to some of the carved areas using oil pastel. Work the pastel into an area using a cosmetic sponge or your gloved finger.

14

It's never too late to go back and create additional texture with your carving tools. This is a great way to add some white areas if desired.

15

I use PanPastels to work on shadowing and add highlights in certain areas. The color is applied with a sponge and stays put better than soft pastels.

16

You can add pops of specific color or add linear detail with the acrylic paint markers. If you sort of "pounce" gently on the tip of the marker, it will create a splat on your piece that is often interesting.

I started these pieces side by side, with a composition that spanned both pieces. During the process, I frequently turned them and worked in all four directions. Working abstract paintings this way can lead to more interesting results.

What's in Your Pantry?

No clayboard? Don't despair; grab whatever substrate you have on hand such as watercolor paper or canvas. Simply skip over the carving part of the project and proceed as indicated. Another alternative is to substitute water-soluble pencils or crayons—even water-soluble oil pastels. Instead of blending the pencils with water, use matte medium. Or try wetting your paper first with matte medium (or gesso) and draw into it or sand bits of watercolor pencil over your wet substrate. Sprinkle with kosher salt.

Guest Artist:
Sarah Ahearn Bellemare

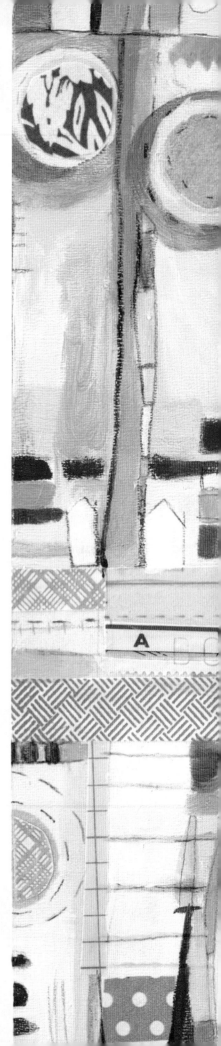

Fresh is the first word that comes to mind when seeing the art of Sarah Ahearn Bellemare. While growing up in western Massachusetts, Sarah spent every summer on the ocean in Cape Cod. This memory is reflected in her work today in the light and airy colors of her delightfully whimsical work.

Always creative as a child, Sarah is like many of us in that she didn't think she was good enough to be an artist and thus originally sought a career in art therapy, hoping that might be the next best direction. One thing led to another, and today she not only enjoys an active teaching career but displays her work in several galleries, and she has just signed a book contract. She and her husband have just had their first child, and Sarah rejoices in the fact they recently moved back near both sets of family.

Like many artists, Sarah keeps a sketchbook but describes it as "quirky" in that she often has to search past the to-do lists to find tidbits of inspiration. In fact, she has a number of sketchbooks that she refers to as collections—collages of things she wants to remember.

She navigates back and forth from custom dog portraits to other mixed media such as text-inspired work for a recent gallery show. Currently she is working on a series with old family photos, using a lot of image transfers. When making her work, she likes to be surrounded by all her materials and grab little bits from here and there as they might appeal or speak to her. She says, "The materials tell me where to go."

She proves my point about process in that her approach toward cooking is similar. Having worked at a number of high-end restaurants, Sarah is particular about both the taste of the food and the artistic presentation of the meal. She is currently into Mexican food, specifically condiments and the idea of lots of little things from which to choose. She delights in a simple dish like fish tacos surrounded by tiny mismatched bowls full of topping choices. I have no doubt this is a feast for the eyes, just like her artwork!

Triad Color Theory

I have enjoyed Sarah's work for a long time, and it only recently occurred to me that she uses a palette of primary colors: red, yellow and blue (and lots of white). And oh, how lovely it is.

When I first started to paint, I would get so excited that I used nearly every tube of paint I could get my hands on in each and every painting. As you might imagine, I created lots of mud. Add to that, I used them right out of the tube, so I had few value changes, certainly no shades—no tints. I became incredibly frustrated with my results and decided I should spend some time learning about color.

Color theory, in its most complex form, can be mind-numbing. I mean everyone has heard about the primary colors—red/yellow/blue—but try working with them! Geez, I experimented for a long time before I found mixes that really worked. It seemed like I could never find the right red to mix with the right blue. After lots and lots of experimentation, I can now save you some trouble! Join me as I get specific and demonstrate how you can produce different palette options to suit your mood.

The only true way to become familiar with color is to actually paint and play with the colors yourself. I am giving you an example of some triads (one color from the red family, one in the yellow category and a third in some form of blue) that I use often, but obviously I don't use these exclusively.

Pick out triads of your own, mix colors, make color wheels—see what happens when you mix complementary colors. You will learn so much—trust me.

Here are some triads that I use:

First is the earthy choice:
Yellow Ochre/Burnt Sienna/Payne's Gray

Next up, a good all-around triad:
Quinacridone Nickel Azo Gold/Quinacridone Red/Prussian Blue

And finally, the bright and perky choice:
Hansa Yellow/Quinacridone Magenta/Phthalo Blue (green shade)

When I am painting in my studio, I use a deli sheet as my palette paper. I typically limit my palette to see how many colors I can mix. I use only two of the primaries at a time (addition of the third will guarantee mud) and add white or black. I keep mixing and mixing all over the page. When my day of painting is complete, I make a note of what colors I used and glue the deli sheet into my Palette Page Journal. It makes a very nice reference.

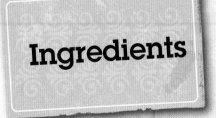

Ingredients

→ Select a triad from the sample list. You can use fluid- or heavy-bodied acrylic—just stick with all the same kind within the triad.
→ palette paper or deli sheet
→ Titanium White
→ smallish bristle brush
→ watercolor paper, 140 lb. (300gsm) is good—any size
→ paper cutter, scissors or ruler, craft knife and cutting mat
→ glue stick
→ cardstock

1 Squeeze a bit of each color onto your palette paper, plus Titanium White.

2 Paint one of the colors onto your watercolor page. Mix white with it and paint a dab of the new color on your page.

3 Keep mixing and painting, making combinations of only two of the three primary colors. Vary the ratios of each pair of colors—you don't need equal amounts of each. Mix each with white, and the resulting colors with white. See how many colors you can make. Do not mix all three primary colors or you will make mud.

4 Continue colors together and adding strokes of these combos to your paper. Also experiment with how the colors layer over one another with a bit of water added to your brush. When you feel you have exhausted enough combinations and have filled up your paper, you will have a nice range of possibilities and should have a pretty good feel for how these paints perform together.

5 It is fun to take this experiment one step further and make a mosaic. Begin by cutting your dried paper into many squares. I like my squares to be the same size, but you can use different sizes if you like.

6 Then glue the pieces in a grid-like pattern onto a new piece of paper, and you will have a wonderful glance of your palette. It looks way cooler than a color wheel.

What's in Your Pantry?

The triads that I use are simply suggestions; you will likely find many more that you want to try. For instance, if you want an earthy palette but would like a wider range of blues, use Prussian Blue instead of Payne's Gray. Earthy with a lighter feel? Substitute Cerulean Blue for Payne's Gray or Quinacridone Gold for Yellow Ochre. If you want earthy but prefer more red, use Cadmium Red instead of Burnt Sienna. The main object here is to work with the colors frequently enough so you gain familiarity with how they act. If you want to really limit your palette and challenge yourself even further, try using black instead of your blue. (Yes this can work.)

Palette pages are excellent reference tools and serve as realistic examples of exactly what happens when mixing color.

Sometimes color play can result in an actual painting, such as the framed pieces here. I worked these pieces in a very free-form way, painting imaginary shapes.

Guest Artist: Elizabeth MacCrellish

One of the most authentic people I have ever met is Elizabeth MacCrellish, who was in the first class I taught at Artfest. Sometimes you just get lucky, huh? Had she not been in my class, I might have missed meeting her, and what a shame that would have been.

Despite a childhood interest in visual art and memories of the art smock her cousins in France sent, Elizabeth has always been a writer. Although she did a gig in corporate America, before founding Squam Art Workshops, she was teaching English and French literature at the New Hampshire Institute of Art where she is still adjunct faculty. When asked how Squam Art Workshops came about, Elizabeth says simply, "Because I went to Artfest and got cracked open." She goes on to explain that when attending Artfest, she felt for the first time that she had found her tribe. She also credits Artfest with giving her permission to make two-dimensional art.

Returning to New Hampshire, her dream of creating an art center somehow transformed into Squam. The first year, she attracted 135 people from twenty-seven states. Flash forward to her third year and she now offers five different sessions, which appeal to all types of seekers from artists to performers to writers.

Her current artwork explores gourds and the female figure because of their earth and goddess energy. Her work is passionate and organic. The parallels between her art-making and cooking processes are infinite. She likes to start with a theme and let the creativity unfold from there. She revels in the simpler parts of the process, such as washing vegetables. For Elizabeth, process is the most important thing, be it cooking or art making. And she says that cooking is like painting in that she never does it the same way twice.

For a recent dinner, she experimented with Bourguignon by substituting portobello mushrooms and transforming the French dish into a vegetarian treat. Her guests were delighted (the vegetarians especially!). Elizabeth has a way of making each and every person she encounters feel very special—a talent far surpassing her brilliance in writing, art or cooking.

Elizabeth's Favorite
Recipe for: Squash Soup with Chipotle

- 1 Blue Hubbard squash
- 3 T. olive oil
- ½ cup chopped onion
- a bit of fresh celery leaves, minced
- 1 garlic clove, mashed
- 4–6 cups stock (veggie, chicken or turkey)
- 2 chipotles in adobo (dried are also OK)
- ½ cup sour cream
- salt, freshly ground pepper

→ Preheat oven to 400°F (204°C). Remove seeds from the squash and cut into pieces. Place the pieces cut-side down on a shallow baking tray that has about an inch of water in it. Roast the pieces about 35 to 40 minutes or until tender. Let cool.

→ Heat the oil in a large, heavy pot over medium high. Sauté the onion and celery until transparent. Add the garlic; cook a few minutes more. Add the chopped chipotle. Scoop the flesh of the squash into the pot and stir. Season with salt and pepper. Add 4 cups of broth and simmer, covered, for 30 minutes and then let sit overnight, covered in the fridge. This isn't necessary, but the soup is always better when given time to sit.

→ Heat on the stove on low as you puree the soup in batches in a blender or using an immersion blender. Add sour cream at the end to get the desired consistency. Ladle into bowls and garnish with toasted seeds, cilantro, sour cream or whatever you desire.

Organic Abstract Painting

The abstract that we worked on earlier in this chapter was very linear and geometric. Elizabeth's work is quite different with its flowing shapes and curving lines that reference nature. So let's switch gears and try our hand at an organic approach. Think about shapes of leaves and rocks and flowers and gourds—free-flowing shapes like circles and spirals.

We will work on canvas so you can see the different effects achieved with the ink. We will also use alcohol inks this time. And then we will play with invented writing and scribble on the face of the painting to try to evoke a more accidental look.

Ingredients

- stretched canvas or canvas panel, any size
- collage pieces
- gel medium
- bristle brushes
- acrylic paint
- acrylic ink
- spray bottles—one with water, one with alcohol
- paper towels
- hair dryer
- alcohol ink
- Sharpie Mean Streak marker or Marvy Permanent ID Stick
- oil pastel
- black gel or glaze pen
- china marker

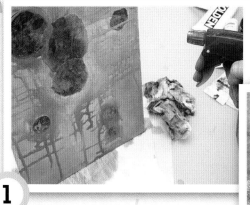

1 Start by collaging found papers onto the canvas, being sure to brush acrylic medium over the top of the collaged parts. I used paper with a textured appearance that I had torn into circular shapes. Using fluid acrylic paint, apply a thin coat over the entire piece. When dry, apply acrylic artist ink using the dropper from the ink bottle.

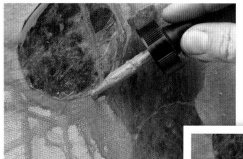

2 Spritz with water and allow the watery ink to run and drip on the piece. Turn the piece, if desired, to make the ink run in multiple directions.

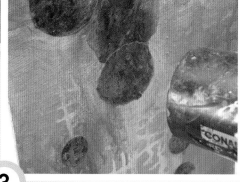

3 Dry with the hair dryer and then gently wipe the canvas in some spots, using a paper towel. You will see white is revealed where the ink had previously dripped!

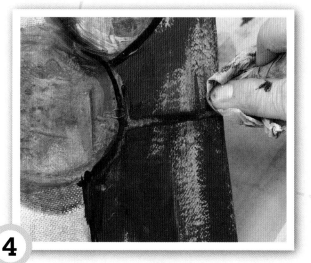

4 Repeat this process with additional colors. Sometimes I go back and add in more acrylic paint as well. Here I bumped up the green and blue some more, added in some Burnt Sienna, then created more drips with two more earth tones. Now, instead of spritzing with water, wait until the ink is almost dry, then rub it off with a paper towel. Only outlines of the drips will remain, which looks really cool.

5 Apply alcohol ink to some areas, and either spread the color around a bit or else let it drip. The alcohol ink gives a vibrant effect that lends a nice contrast.

6 Spritz over the inked areas with alcohol. Spray generously, and move the canvas in different directions to let the alcohol pick up and move the paint around.

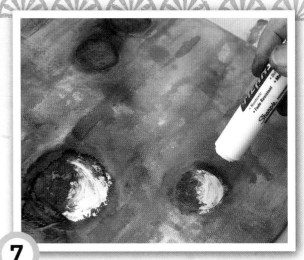

7 Continue adding and dripping inks until you are satisfied. If you want to add some white back, you can draw with a Sharpie Mean Streak marker. This dries quickly, but you have a few seconds to work it in with your finger. Here I wanted to add some highlights in my circles.

8 Sharpen some details with some black. Here I'm using oil pastel.

9 It's also fun to use black pen to add very fine details. My favorite three (which all write very nicely on dry acrylics) are a china marker, Uniball Vision and Sakura Glaze.

What's in Your Pantry?

Try an organic-feeling abstract in a very limited palette. Use an all-over type of composition—circles on top of circles, draw them free form, all sizes and shapes—and cover your canvas, as if you are looking at a bunch of pebbles on the bottom of a lake. Or use a large spiral shape and then do your scribble writing within its edges. Imagine tree branches as you would view them lying on the ground or cloud shapes . . . I feel a series coming on!

Minimalistic work, whether a
limited palette or simple composition, can be evocative.
In these pieces, the drips are
used to create linear detail and
invite the viewer to step closer.

TEXTURE

For me, the most successful texture is that which invites the viewer to touch the painting—something considered a no-no in most art venues. I remember a particular Rauschenberger painting (called *Collection*, formerly untitled, 1954) at the San Francisco Museum of Modern Art. I loved to stand in front of that painting visually exploring the impasto strokes layered on top of collage elements including wood, fabric and well, pieces of junk. The piece was so painterly that it taunted me, causing an ache inside that made me want to achieve similar power within my own work. Ultimately, it made me want to run home and grab my paintbrush so I could play with creating thick, dense brushstrokes.

Artists Shari Beaubien, Susan Tuttle and Laura Lein-Svencner join us in our discussion of texture. Their works are as diverse as the women, and they inspired me in different directions too. I will show the two types of texture I use in my work—that which is carved into the piece and that which is added onto the piece. We'll make a Clayboard Book, a Candle Shade and a Texture Sampler. We will carve and cut, crackle and paste, mold and glue. Let's get started!

The true worth of a man **is not to be found in man himself, but in the colours and textures that come alive in others.**
—Albert Schweitzer

Guest Artist: Shari Beaubien

From theater major to hairstylist to aerobics instructor to calligrapher, Shari Beaubien has worked at a number of careers, but says that making art has allowed her to "come home to who I am." A self-described perfectionist, she has worked as a professional artist since 2004. Her strong work ethic has guided her to achieve success in a variety of areas, from art fairs to teaching to gallery shows. She has recently signed with a publishing house, so her work is available for licensing.

Although she has taken workshops and college-level art classes, Shari is proud of being self-taught and enjoys the freedom of being able to explore every whim or avenue that she wants without limitation. Simply put, she strives to evolve as an artist. In the short term, she looks to expand her gallery presence and secure licensing contracts. Her dream is to someday write and illustrate a children's book.

Super-creative as a child, Shari is glad she has found her way to art as an adult. She maintains a strong discipline, trying to paint nearly every day, especially early when the light is good. She cherishes "the quiet time between me and the paint." Her process involves acrylic on canvas, building surface texture and then using ink and graphite along with paint. She has gotten away from collage to some extent, preferring to paint her own imagery and characters for each of her series.

She has recently adopted a vegan diet and is interested in developing a lifestyle that is more simplistic, from a commitment to eating local foods to living with pared-down possessions. Interestingly, she has found that her paintings have simultaneously migrated to a more simplistic look, with what she describes as "less noise."

Shari and her husband enjoy good food, and Shari credits the Food TV network as her teacher. Curiously, this perfectionist confesses she hates to measure and prefers to figure out the recipe on her own rather than follow the directions. I am betting this is because she comes up with something better than the original recipe.

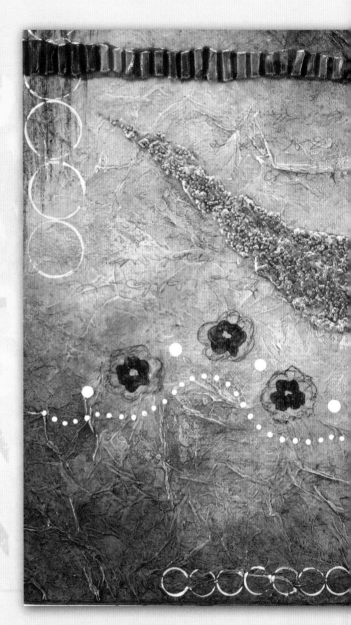

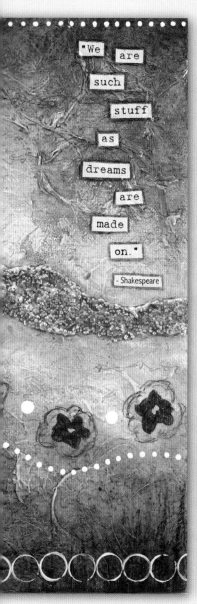

"We are such stuff as dreams are made on."

- Shakespeare

S. Beaubrier

Clayboard Book

In ancient times, a diptych was a hinged writing tablet or an altarpiece. A diptych, like Shari has made, is two paintings that are displayed as one. Although I often make paintings that consist of multiple panels, I have to be honest and admit that I didn't even think of using my paintings for book covers until a friend suggested it to me (thanks, Karyl!). Of course, she is a bookbinder, and I am a painter, so go figure.

Anyway, there is something absolutely incredible about assembling clayboard paintings into a book. Clayboard makes the covers feel beefy and important and, well, so hardbound. I use simple binder rings for assembly because I like my books to be functional and flexible enough to add and subtract pages at will. Alternatively, you could bind this "for real" using a coptic stitch or stab binding. Do what works for you. Now let's grab some power tools and check out the texture opportunities.

Ingredients

- clayboard, 2 smooth, same-size flat panels
- pencil
- rotary tool (such as a Dremel) with ⅛" (3mm) drill bit and grinding stone attachment
- engraving tool (Dremel)
- Fiber Paste, Clear Tar Gel and Glass Bead Gel (Golden)
- palette knife
- stencils
- wooden skewer
- bristle brushes
- acrylic paint
- Mr. Clean Magic Eraser
- small Claybord scraps (optional) (Ampersand)
- craft glue
- black glaze pen or gel pen
- binder rings
- assorted paper, cut to size of clayboards

1 Start with two clayboards that are the same size. Sketch out a rough composition with pencil. Along the two sides that will be the spine, drill three holes, using an ⅛" (3mm) drill bit. My holes are about ¼" (6mm) from the edge, with one hole centered and the other two 1" (3cm) from the top and bottom.

2 Lightly sketch out a word, then, using an engraving tool, carve out the letters. Use the engraving tool to also carve other sections as desired.

3 I love to create circles using the end of a rotary tool grinding stone—you need to hold the tool firmly and bring it straight down onto the surface. Practice first on a scrap piece of clayboard or on the back of the piece.

4 When you are finished carving, begin applying mediums as a base for more texture. I like to apply Fiber Paste using a palette knife. I just spread it around and leave nice big strokes showing.

Got You Covered

It is a matter of personal preference whether you line up the front and back cover when you draw your composition. Sometimes I love the look of a continued line, but other times I create each cover somewhat separate from the other. I do try to keep the palette consistent so it looks like the covers actually go together.

5 Glass Bead Gel works well through stencils. Here I am using punchanella.

6 Tar gel is fun to apply using a wooden skewer. Drizzle it on, creating loose shapes with the drizzle. You can also draw with it (to some extent) using the end of the skewer.

7 Allow the mediums to dry before you begin painting the boards. I like to start my painting by section. I first put down a coat of Titanium Buff. Then I start layering color. I like to switch back and forth between the heavier-bodied acrylics and the fluid acrylics. Although I tend to use my pencil lines as a guide, I sometimes change my mind and paint over them.

8 A Magic Eraser is a cool tool for bringing back white areas. Dampen it with water and rub it over raised or flat areas. It will remove paint back down to the original color of the clayboard.

Consider Your Values

One thing I always keep in mind when creating my pieces is to try to imagine how they would look if copied in black and white. If it seems like they would turn out looking all mid-range gray, I lighten my lights and darken my darks in order to add some interest and contrast. Imagining your piece as black and white is an easy way to see if you have value changes represented in your work.

9 Continue layering dark and light colors, laying color down, wiping it away, laying more down. Sometimes I like to drybrush more concentrated color over part of the raised textured areas.

10 Another way to add dimension is with a shape that is glued on. Here I have added a 1" (3cm) Claybord square. Add final details using a black pen such as a glaze pen.

11 Assemble the book by punching holes through your chosen paper. Be sure to line everything up so your paper holes match up with your cover holes, then thread a binder ring through the two covers and paper at each hole.

What's in Your Pantry?

Instead of making book covers, simply alter existing ones. Old discarded books make excellent painting substrates. Many older books have a cloth covering that is similar to canvas. If the book is in poor condition, I think you are honoring it by transforming it into a painting.

Or, to make an altarpiece, scrounge flea markets for an item that is hinged or will stand up on its own. Think shutters, gameboards, notebooks, picture frames, fireplace screens—you get the idea. Lightly sand the item first and then create your new painting on top, either completely covering the image below or allowing some of it to peek through.

Guest Artist:
Susan Tuttle

Multisensory expression must come easily to Susan Tuttle because her artistic journey, first as a musician, then as a visual artist, is simply amazing. From the age of nine, playing the flute has always allowed her to connect with her creative spirit. She followed this tune through college and went on to teach elementary school music, all the while fostering her love for visual art by spending time in museums and making crafty things during her summers off.

A car accident ultimately caused her to reassess her life, and she found herself with the sudden need to express herself through charcoal drawings. When she and her husband moved to Maine in 1999, she started painting acrylic abstracts and then migrated into mixed media. One day, her husband told her about an NPR show he heard explaining artist trading cards. After exploring them online, Susan found an entirely new community of people and Web sites and blogs, and that is when she first learned of *Somerset Studio* magazine. One thing led to another as she moved from mixed media to assemblage to photography and digital art—all the while continuing as a musician, writing a popular blog, teaching online and writing two books. In a word, she is a dynamo.

Susan's home is in rural Maine farm country, surrounded by an intersection of rivers, an area I imagine to be as idyllic and unspoiled as her work. Her usual routine includes hiking on their acreage over many trails that link up nearby properties. This connection with nature is one of many things that inspire her work.

When thinking about art and life, Susan believes that "to indulge all senses is art." Thus, she loves to eat, especially good food, which is a treat she and her husband enjoy on occasion at an upscale restaurant. She has a memory of special dinners growing up when her parents took their family to The Frog and the Peach restaurant, an event where she first learned to savor food.

And yes, as you might have guessed, she has a share in a local CSA (Community Supported Agriculture), which allows her to indulge her family in healthy local eats on a regular basis.

No matter what Susan pursues, she does it with such complete passion and joy that it affects all those around her positively, which is a lovely legacy.

Susan's Approach to Eating

I enjoy combining a variety of flavors in my meals—"layers of flavor" so to speak. For lunch there is often simple, rustic food to waken and dazzle my sense of taste: grilled asparagus, fresh juicy tomato, good mozzarella—thinly sliced, sweet crispy onion with basil and olive oil drizzled on top and a slice of hearty peasant bread to complement the snack. I enjoy the individual tastes and textures and the many combinations of flavors playing off of each other, swirling around in my mouth. This is not unlike my passion for digital art, where I combine layers of imagery and texture and apply blending modes to a variety of these layers, allowing the tonal aspects of the imagery to play off of one another.

Texture Sampler

Susan's digital layers are mysterious and moody. Although there is no actual touchable texture, there is implied texture. An artist creates implied texture when the visual effect of texture is achieved despite the fact the piece is two-dimensional. Simply said, you can see texture in the piece, but you can't feel it.

We are going to create both types of texture in this next project, making a sampler that is reminiscent of old-time embroidery pieces.

What's in Your Pantry?

Make a texture journal. First, using thin paper and a soft lead pencil, collect a variety of rubbings. Then make sample pages of all other kinds of texture you have used in the past. From acrylic mediums to impasto paint to clay to embedded items (think grass, wood shavings, safety glass), work up as many textures as you can. Assemble all your pages into a journal, and you will have an amazing reference tool for texture, both implied and real.

Make your own implied texture papers. Grab some fat crayons or pencils (look in the children's section of the art store). Using any type of thin paper, start a collection of cool rubbings in a variety of colors, and keep them on hand for future mixed-media pieces.

Ingredients

- tracing paper
- pencil or graphite crayon (soft lead is best)
- rigid substrate (I am using a Masonite panel)
- gesso
- textures for rubbing
- gel medium
- bristle brushes
- glue
- variety of acrylic texture mediums, including Glass Bead Gel (Golden) (optional)
- Wood Icing Textura (optional)
- variety of acrylic paints
- stencils
- spray varnish

1 Using tracing paper and a very soft pencil, go around your house, studio or yard and find textures for creating rubbings—the type you did when you were a kid. All you do is place the paper on top of the surface and gently rub using the side of the lead of the pencil. These rubbings are implied texture. Then, once you have some rubbings, begin by applying gesso to your substrate and allow to dry. Sand lightly, then gesso again. Sand once more until the substrate is smooth.

2 Glue rubbings to your substrate. Now apply some acrylic texture mediums to your substrate (I used Wood Icing with a stencil and Glass Bead Gel). Allow to dry and then sand lightly if desired.

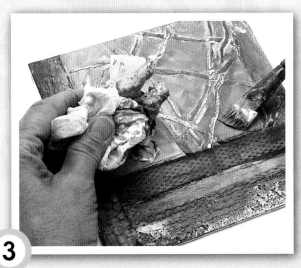

3 Start painting with acrylic paints to bring out the texture. I am using Cerulean Blue, Yellow Ochre, Titanium White and Transoxide Yellow.

4 Continue painting and embellishing until you are satisfied. Add additional collage elements or rubbings to your piece if you wish. I finished off with a glossy spray varnish.

Prep Work

There are a lot of boards and panels on the market today, not to mention all the options you can find at your local hardware store. I enjoy working on all kinds of substrates, and sometimes I simply prefer a rigid surface—think Masonite, hardboard or MDF, which is really just pressed board. If a panel doesn't come pre-gessoed, it's a good idea to lay down several coats of white gesso on the panel in order to prepare it as a painting surface. Sometimes, even if a board comes gessoed, I will still put a coat of my own gesso on it because I don't always care for the plastic quality of the manufactured gesso.

Guest Artist:
Laura Lein-Svencner

Laura Lein-Svencner is an Internet pal whom I finally met in person at an art fair last year. Having only seen her work online, I was blown away by the richness she achieves with the Jonathan Talbot method of collage (using an iron). She has truly mastered his technique and made it her own by utilizing hand-painted papers to create soulful textured works that often are inspired by Native American myth.

Although she has been making things for many years, art has only been a full-time focus for the last ten years. She got serious when she found herself with more time as her kids grew older and better able to take care of themselves. Her work varies from collage to painted reclaimed skateboards to assemblage works. She creates in series, finding inspiration in a variety of areas, but especially through nature.

These days, Laura is an absolute frenzy of activity, teaching classes in several locations, as well as exhibiting in art fairs and galleries. She keeps herself grounded with daily nature walks, journal writing and by being in her home.

Typically, her art-making process starts with paper preparation, either making new painted papers or selecting from her vast collection—stored hanging from a garment rack so she can easily see her options (a storage tip one of her students shared with her).

She will often stew about the work until something bubbles up from inside and she knows she can "re-create the feeling" through collage. While working on her present series, Laura referred back to her original inspiration, the children's book *Thirteen Moons on Turtle's Back*. Then, trusting color as a guide, she allowed her instincts to guide her direction and help her capture the legend.

Laura readily admits she isn't cooking as much as she used to, but her family still loves it when she makes homemade flour tortillas. The process of gathering and sharing is evident in Laura's work and also echoed in her feelings about cooking for her family. Clearly she infuses her spirit into everything she does.

Laura's Family Favorite, *Flour Tortillas*

Recipe for:

→ 4 cups white flour
→ 1 tsp. salt
→ ¼ tsp. baking powder
→ ¾–1 cup oil
→ 1 cup warm water

→ Add all dry ingredients together. Pour in oil and water. Mix well and knead gently. Divide dough into 12 to16 balls. Cover and let rest for 15 to 20 minutes.

→ First hand knead the dough ball, then roll out on an unfloured counter with a rolling pin, spreading the dough as round and thin as you can to about 7" to 9" diameter. Heat an ungreased skillet (cast-iron if you have it). Gently place one tortilla in the skillet. Watch for air bubbles and poke down; flip over when you see little brown speckles appear. Cook on both sides. Keep warm on plate under a towel. The tortillas store well in the fridge or freezer.

No day but today

Candle Shade

For years I have been itching to make a painterly item that is also practical. Part of this interest comes from my participation in art fairs. In times of a slow economy, two-dimensional paintings are not exactly a big drawing card, but despite my best efforts, I could never think of a way to turn a painting into something that was actually functional.

Something about Laura's piece inspired me to move in a new direction. I found her composition interesting in that it loosely reminded me of a stencil I had designed. I adored her rich color selection and subtle texture along with slight metallic points of interest. These ideas somehow merged together and inspired me to create this cute little Candle Shade.

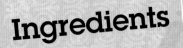

Ingredients

- canvas panels, 3 same size
- pencil
- rotary tool (Dremel) with multipurpose cutting and grinding stone attachments
- paintbrushes
- acrylic paint
- Hard Molding Paste (Golden)
- stencil
- palette knife
- black ink
- gold thermal foil
- tacking iron
- Apoxie Clay
- craft knife
- hand drill
- candle, real or battery powered

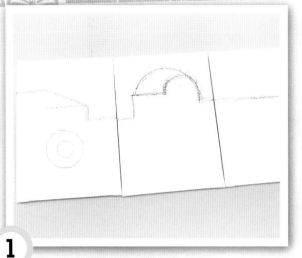

1 Start by sketching out how the top will be shaped. Remember that all three sides will be joined, so your drawing should connect across the panels.

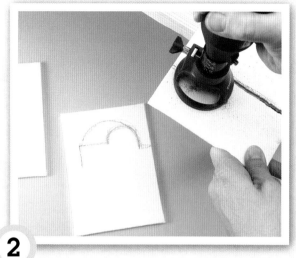

2 Cut out the shape using a saw or multipurpose tool.

3 Sand the edges of the sawed shapes using a sanding block, file or rotary tool.

4 Paint both sides of all pieces with black acrylic paint. Let dry.

5 Apply hard molding paste across each of the panels using a stencil and a palette knife. Be mindful of the design carrying through all three pieces so they are joined when connected. Set aside to dry.

6 Using heavy-bodied acrylics, begin adding color to the molding paste. Here I wanted to keep the feeling light, so I kept the colors to Yellow Ochre, Titanium Buff and Quinacridone Gold. Also, I wanted to preserve the black, so I tried to use a somewhat dry brush and limit the color to the molding paste areas.

7 To add some depth, I brushed on a bit of black ink around the edges of the molding paste "tiles."

8 Add of bit of sparkle with some hot-pressed gold foil. Without trying to cover the entire surface, use an iron to apply heat, and the foil will fuse to areas where there is paste.

Can't Resist Stencils?

I use a stencils a lot—so much so that I have even created my own stenciling products. Even so, I still love to improvise, and anything that has cut out parts is interesting to me, like lace or a doily or die-cut scrapbook supplies. I use them with both paints and texture pastes. To protect delicate things (like doilies or paper items), I first spray them on both sides with spray paint. Usually one or two coats will provide enough protection when using paint or medium. You can simply wipe them off with a damp paper towel to clean.

9 Check your progress and add more foil if desired. Alternatively, you could use traditional metallic leaf and adhesive.

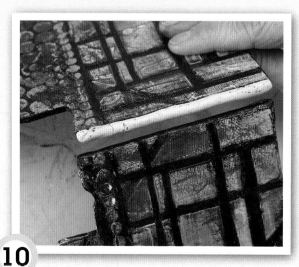

10 Following manufacturer's instructions, mix up a small amount of Apoxie clay and form it into a snake. Press the first two sides of the structure together.

11 When all three sides are pushed together, clean up the excess clay using a craft knife.

12 Paint the clay black. Set aside to cure for the recommended amount of time. Drill a series of holes using a hand or power drill; this will allow light to shine through.

13

Touch up the holes with paint and set a candle inside.

What's in Your Pantry?

Using Apoxie Clay and canvas board, I think you could make just about anything. You could make another Candle Shade in a different shape, such as a house. Try making a box or functional items for your office: an in/out tray or magazine storage bin or a sturdy portfolio or notebook. The sky is the limit; use existing items as templates to make your own patterns.

Photo by Greg Barth

These pieces, both done on clay-board, make use of clay elements such as spirals, circles and linear details. The Greek key design was done with Wood Icing and a stencil.

Photo by Greg Barth

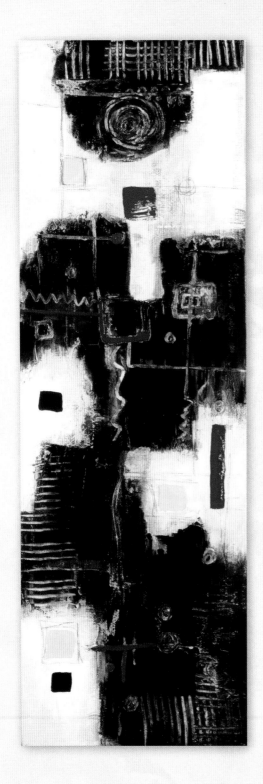

Photos by Greg Barth

To create this pair of abstracts, I used Wood Icing and scribbled into it with a skewer. There are many layers of paint and some of the scribbling exposes layers underneath.

Photo by Greg Barth

On this shrine, I used Apoxie Clay to create textured edges. I also made little clay balls and leaves to accentuate the design.

LAYERS

There is no way to fake layers. Although I repeat this often in classes, truly I don't know why you would want to, because this is such a fun part of the mixed-media process—the creation of multiple layers that add complexity to the work. Years ago, I was featured in a local magazine. It was an unexpected treat; a reporter had seen my work and decided to write a little review, unbeknownst to me. The title of the article was "Layers of Meaning." That has always stuck in my head. I was so thrilled that he "got it," and I even started to use the phrase as a tagline of sorts.

For me, the layers are absolutely vital. With each and every one, we have an opportunity to transform the appearance and/or meaning of a piece. This can be done in subtle ways through transparent layers, or through more obvious methods. Guest artists Julie Snidle, Tonia Davenport and Dolan Geiman have provided work to influence the approach. We will learn how to make our own papers (for layering) by making layered Collagraph Plate. We will also explore two ways to make three-dimensional paintings, with Plexiglas and Claybord. It's going to be fun because, well, with layers, the more, the merrier.

Layer by layer, **art strips life bare.**
—Robert Musil

Guest Artist:
Julie Snidle

Julie Snidle describes her art as a passion that has always been an important hobby limited only by the lack of time she experienced while raising her girls. Now that they are nearly grown, she is ready to ramp up her commitment to artistic endeavors. Her appetite for learning is voracious, and she has expertly designed the perfect home-based studio from which she works.

Growing up a shy kid in a large high school, Julie felt intimidated by art class when she was younger. She always felt that the "real artists" were a predetermined group of which she was not a member. Knowing Julie personally, I can attest that she is not shy anymore. (In fact, between you and me, it seems laughable to think of her that way.) Her interest in art and her experience level have blossomed over the years.

She has taken classes in a variety of topics, moving from rubber stamps to watercolor to encaustic. She has an admirable level of self-discipline and challenges herself with assignments to make things such as a gift for her dad's eightieth birthday party or a donation for a local fundraiser. Seeing one of her donated works sold at auction for $400 has given her confidence in her abilities, and she thinks it would be interesting to take her art to the next level—meaning back to school, a step she is considering.

The physicality of the medium is interesting to her. In fact, she usually starts a piece by first picking the medium. She embraces the chance to play and finds that she experiments a lot more these days than when she started. This sense of experimentation does not tranfer to cooking. She laughs when admitting that she follows a recipe to a T.

But with art, it is different, and she is on a journey to find her artistic voice. As somewhat of a perfectionist, she wonders if perfection and art can live in the same world. She respects the loose watercolor work of John Singer Sargent and Charles Reid and studies this work at length. She thinks that art is helping her learn to not sweat the small stuff, like overcoming her need to color inside the lines.

Recipe for Fun

Consider hosting a Paper Luncheon with friends as my friend Julie Snidle did. She invited a group of us over to her house, and we each made a collagraph plate. We took a break for lunch to allow the plates to dry thoroughly, and after lunch, we were "printing maniacs." We pulled prints from our own plates as well as each other's. By the end of the day, I had a lovely stash of papers.

...very good luck, every little kindness, every thoughtful action which comes from a heart full of faith has a way of blessing the giver and multiplying the gift.

Collagraph Plate

I enjoy making hand-painted papers to use in my collages. I like the option of using my own paint palette to create papers that I know will match my work. It is especially nice to have a selection of papers on hand from which to choose. Printmaking makes it really easy to build a paper supply quickly.

For this project, we will make a texture collage on a rigid substrate. This collage will serve as a printing plate for a process called collagraphy—which basically means using a collage to make prints. The prints themselves are called collagraphs. Big word, easy process. We are doing it all by hand using acrylic paints, so no extra expensive equipment is needed.

Ingredients

- mat board or other heavy board to use as a substrate
- pieces with texture
- gel medium
- glue brush (you may also want to wear gloves)
- stencils
- Wood Icing (see Resources) or Heavy Molding Paste (Golden)
- palette knife
- sanding block
- acrylic paints
- glass or plexi sheet for palette
- extender medium (to extend drying time)
- brayer
- paper
- spray bottle with water

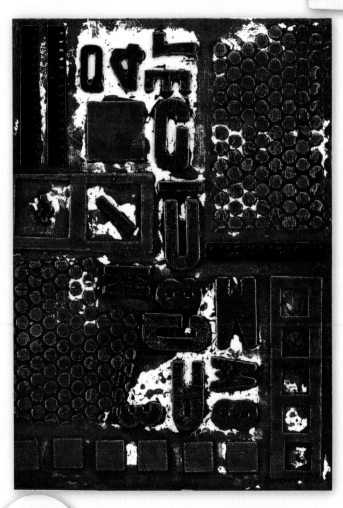

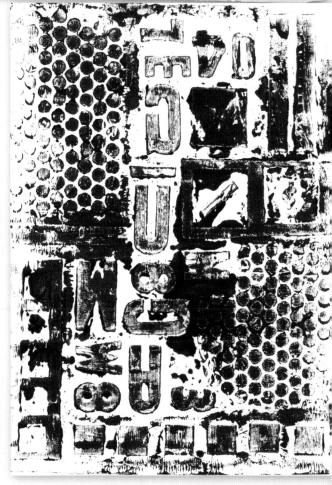

1 Start with a piece of mat board as your plate surface. Begin gluing down elements using the gel medium. It is best if all your pieces are approximately the same height. As you are developing your piece, keep in mind that the print will come out as a reverse. This may or may not make a difference to you; in this example, I am using letters and numbers and have intentionally reversed some but not others.

2 In addition to gluing pieces, I also like to use stencils and Wood Icing to build shapes of texture. Lay the stencil (sequin waste) down, and using a palette knife, spread the icing over the stencil, leveling it off with the knife on the stencil. Heavy molding paste will also work. Set the plate aside to dry.

3 After the plate is dry, you may want to sand the stenciled areas a bit so the height is even. Brush off any debris. Paint an even coat of gel medium over the entire plate to seal it well. If it seems like the plate is warping, you can also apply a coat of gel medium to the back of the plate.

4 Using your piece of glass as a palette, mix acrylic with some retarder and load up your brayer. Fully ink up the collagraph plate using the brayer.

Paint Preference

I prefer using acrylic paint because of the range of colors available and the fact that the paint is more stable. I have found that prints made using water-soluble printmaking inks are not completely stable; thus the color is reactivated when those papers are used in a collage or painting. You may like that effect, but my painting process is often rather wet, and I simply prefer the color to stay put.

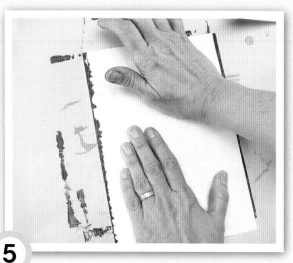

5 Place a piece of paper face down on the inked plate and rub thoroughly with your hands. Try not to move the paper while you are doing this.

6 Peel off the paper to reveal your print. I do not bother to clean the plate, but keep working until I have used up all the paint. Sometimes I will spritz the plate with a little water before making my print. This results in a very different look, which is often beautiful.

What's in Your Pantry?

You don't have to limit yourself to solid-color papers. You can make very interesting prints using ledger pages, old maps or even newspaper. If you don't have time to make a collagraph plate of your own, you can also ink up items from around your house. For instance, the bottoms of shoes frequently have interesting patterns, and old pieces of lace will work, too. A failed painting might also have interesting texture. (Trust me, I have tried it.)

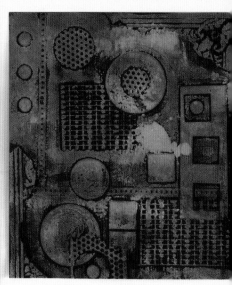

Using black paper (opposite page) creates a dramatic result. I also use deli sheets (above) to make transparent papers. Any type of paper receiving surface will work, but I find I get the best results when I use a light-weight paper.

Guest Artist:
Tonia Davenport

Tonia Davenport readily admits, "I have my dream job." Working for North Light Books as an acquisitions editor, Tonia does seem to have it made. She sees all sorts of art on a daily basis and gets to interact with artists in diverse mediums. I also truly envy her grounded nature, in that she doesn't allow herself to be distracted by the variety of art she sees but simply observes and then continues on her own path. Accordingly, she might not even make art regularly. Instead, she works more sporadically, allowing herself ample time to also do other things she enjoys, such as reading, volunteer work, knitting and cooking.

Graduating college with a major in visual communications/printing/photography prepared her for an arts career, but Tonia is frank when she admits the idea of creating daily under the pressure of a deadline "scared the heck out of me." She prefers to be in a part of the art business that allows her to use both sides of the brain. For instance, her present job and her previous position (in the framing business) utilize the right and left sides of her brain. And the framing business fueled Tonia's interest in Plexiglas, which led her to write a book on the topic.

Like many folks, Tonia has always wished she could keep an art journal, and until recently, she felt she had fallen short in this area. Between 2009 and 2010, she committed to creating a daily doodle on her iPhone, using the colors red, black and white. The discipline has challenged her to say a lot in very little space, and she feels she is developing her own symbolism. In addition, these pictures, which serve as a visual chronicle of each day, are gaining quite a following as she posts them on Facebook.

Tonia is a Foodie with a capital F. She says that she likes cooking but confesses it's really more about the eating for her. Anyone who follows her on Facebook knows of her morning addiction to coffee or tea and chocolate. She also pegs pizza as her favorite food, wood-fired topping her list of the best pizza qualities.

She sums up her art and cooking strategy in a surprising way, "I'm very lazy." When asked to explain, she said she will often improvise with materials on hand rather than going to the store or will end up varying perhaps 70 percent of a recipe. She believes her "laziness" makes her a creative problem-solver. What a unique vantage point; now I know why she is also such a brilliant editor.

Recipe for: Tonia's Favorite Pizza

- store-bought pizza shell (Mama Mary's 100% Whole Wheat is my favorite)
- pumpkin butter (apple butter will work)
- 4–5 slices bacon
- ½ sweet onion, diced
- 1 Granny Smith apple, diced (pear is good, too)
- ¾ cup crumbled gorgonzola cheese
- ¾ cup Quattro Formaggio cheese blend (Trader Joe's)
- 2 T. olive oil

* Preheat oven to 450°F (232°C).

* Top the shell with a layer of pumpkin butter. Fry the bacon in skillet until crisp and drain on paper towels. Reserve about 2 tablespoons drippings in the pan, add olive oil and onion and cook over medium-low heat until onions are caramelized (about 15 minutes). Add the apple to the pan and cook 2 minutes until apples are slightly soft.

* Spread the onion/apple mixture over the shell. Crumble the bacon and spread it and both cheeses over the shell. Bake in hot oven for 8 to 10 minutes or until cheese begins to brown.

Plexi Squared

I have always been intrigued by sheer layering and the opportunity to have parts showing through from underneath other parts. For most of my art life, I have used tissue paper to create this effect, but recently plexi has caught my eye. I love the dimension that can be achieved when working with plexi. Not only is it clear, but it can be raised above the piece to create a quasi three-dimensional effect.

You can ink it, foil it, collage or whatever on it; plexi has more flexibility than you may have imagined. Come along with me as we create a pair of pieces that incorporate plexi.

Ingredients

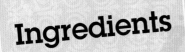

- clayboard, 2 same-size pieces
- gel medium
- paintbrushes
- tissue paper
- sanding block
- collage elements
- scrap plexi and scrap corrugated cardboard
- acrylic and alcohol inks
- spary bottle with alcohol
- fluid acrylics
- paper towels
- craft knife
- black stamp pad
- aluminum foil
- china marker

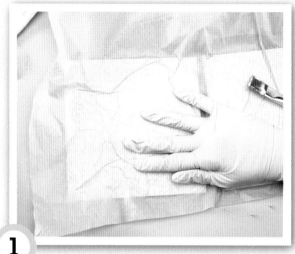

1 Brush gel medium onto a pair of clayboards and press some tissue paper onto the boards.

2 When the medium is dry, use a sanding block against the edge of the board to quickly remove the excess tissue. Add any collage elements that you want using gel medium. Here I am using some strips of sheet music along with pieces of vintage fabric.

3 Cut pieces of plexi or use your own scraps and begin dropping alcohol inks on them.

4 Spritz the ink with straight alcohol and let it run or drip however you like.

5 Continue to work on the plexi and experiment with different colors of alcohol ink to see how they layer over one another to form new colors. Some pieces look nice with fluid acrylic brushed on the back.

6 Additional texture can be created by pressing a paper towel into the wet paint.

7 To create another interesting element, select a piece of scrap corrugated cardboard and adhere an interesting collage element using gel medium.

8 Paint the paper with whatever color(s) you like using a tiny amount of fluid acrylics. Using a craft knife, cut a rectangle shape out of the top layer of the collage paper/ cardboard, being careful not to cut all the way through.

9 Peel off the top layer of paper/cardboard.

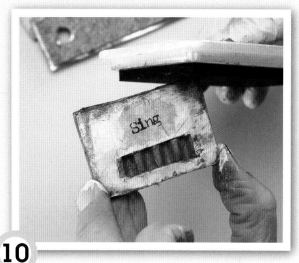

10 Glue a little word onto the cardboard if you like. Then use a black or dark-colored stamp pad to darken the edges.

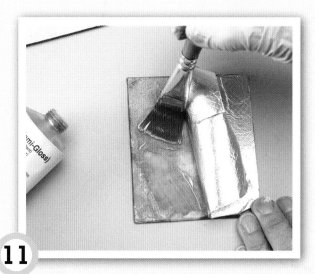

11 One way to make the color on the plexi pop is to adhere aluminum foil to the back of the plexi using gel medium.

Note: I use plain old deli foil, but regular roll aluminum foil also works well. The deli foil has an interesting design that I prefer. They both take alcohol ink perfectly and can be tinted into other interesting metallic tones, such as bronze or gold.

12 I assembled the plexi pieces at different levels on top of the clayboard. Some are simply glued to the clayboard. For the piece shown, I drilled a hole in the plexi, as well as through a wood game piece and secured them to the board with both glue and a copper nail. The drawing on plexi was done with a black china marker.

Finding Plexi

I get plexi scraps from my framer. There are often imperfect spots that render the plexi unsuitable for framing, but it still works fine for my mixed media. If you are going to work with plexi very much, you will want to invest in a scoring tool that is specifically made for plexi. That will make it much easier to score the pieces properly before you break them. A hand drill will also work better for holes.

13 For this piece, I transferred random lettering to foil before adhering it to the plexi.

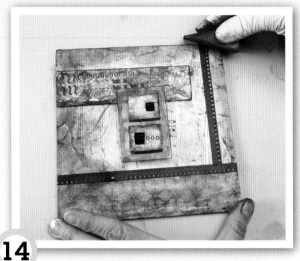

14 Adhere your other pieces with glue or gel medium as well. Finish off the edges to add additional depth using either a stamp pad or PanPastel/sponge.

The second half of this diptych also works well on its own.

Many years ago, I was lucky enough to score some vintage plexi, including the large red O that you see here. After hoarding it forever, I decided it would be a lovely focal point in this piece.

Guest Artist:
Dolan Geiman

One of my favorite things about Dolan Geiman, other than his fabulous art and his wife, Ali, is that he loves caramelized bacon as much as I do. I met Dolan several years ago on the art fair circuit, and I respect his artistic aesthetic so much I was thrilled when he agreed to make a piece for my book.

Originally from the Shenandoah Valley in Virginia, Dolan now calls Chicago home. Dolan recalls, "I remembered a recipe my grandmom used to make when we were little. My mom would say, 'Grandmom is making Rose Compolia tonight.' I never knew what she meant. I always thought it was some strange foreign dish. All I knew was that she said the recipe was from my aunt Pauline.

"Aunt Pauline lived in a huge, white, two-story farm-house with a wraparound porch over on the eastern shore of Virginia. She was bedridden for the time that I knew her, and it was strange to see her this way as a child. I always felt nervous around her, probably because I didn't know what was wrong with her. But all of that nervousness was outweighed by the fact that she always smelled like sweet lotion and roses. So, of course, when I heard the recipe was called Rose Compolia, it made sense to me that it came from the rose-smelling lady.

"All these years later, something made me suddenly think of that dish, and I decided to finally call my grandmother and get the real recipe. Without provocation, she spelled out the recipe name on the card: Pauline Ward's Aroz-Compollo, and it all made sense. Aunt Pauline grew up in Cuba, her mother and father were born there as well, and it wasn't until a missionary family traveled through the area that she was brought to the U.S. It was there she later met my great-uncle Mack Ward, the pig farmer from Pocomoke."

Raised by his artist mother and forest-service father, "making things" was Dolan's primary activity as a child. His family truly did not own a television, and he found himself outdoors most days. A natural scavenger, he recalls sweat-filled balmy days searching the country-side for abandoned properties where he never failed to locate interesting stuff that he carried home.

These days, Dolan continues to scavenge, except now he uses the items in the mixed-media pieces he shows and sells nationally. He gathers materials ranging from vintage doodads to found objects, and all are incorporated into his art. With a true commitment to being "green," all his paint comes from the local recycle center; he even finds use for the "old crusty paint." He finds things in Chicago factories and on Craigslist. As he says, "It's kind of silly to buy new art supplies."

Dolan journals regularly, keeping a number of note-books handy for whenever a thought might strike. He sketches frequently, but also records song lyrics and even presses dead moss. (Clearly, many things are inspirational to his process.)

Although Dolan does not fancy himself as a cook per se, he does throw together the occasional dish, and it invariably involves lots of meat and yep, you guessed it—bacon! Just what you might expect from a good ole southern boy.

Aunt Pauline's Aroz Compollo
(arroz con pollo)

Recipe for: _____

Boil together:
→ 6 or 7 bay leaves
→ ⅛ tsp. caraway seeds
→ 1 diced onion
→ 1 diced green pepper
→ 1 can tomato paste

→ 1 lb. rice, uncooked and washed (my grandmother said they used to recommend people wash their rice, a tradition that has been replaced by today's conveniences)

→ Cook for a few minutes until rice is sort of brown and then add 2 quarts of water.

→ *Optional: a handful of olives and a cup of raisins*

→ When the rice is soft and cooked, pour this all in a large dish. Grandmom said Aunt Pauline would always have some fried chicken cooked and ready to go so she would put the fried chicken on top of this rice mixture. I am sure you could also bake or boil some nice chicken pieces as an alternative to the fried chicken.

Three-Dimensional Painting

You have probably
already figured out that in addition to texture and color, I love my layers. In fact, I dare say I love layers best. This is kinda like picking your favorite kid, but I do love them more than anything else. Carving, texturing, creating with paint, applying dimension to them with plexi and cardboard . . . how I love to layer. So let's move into the third dimension, 'cause this is where it really gets interesting.

With this next project, we will pull out all the stops and create a three-dimensional painting! You don't need special glasses to view it, but I think you'll find it as exciting as if you did. Parts of the painting remain slightly hidden, parts "float" above and some parts cast shadows. So join me as we go ultra-layered working in 3-D.

Ingredients

- pencil
- deep-cradled Claybord (Ampersand)
- standard "flat" claybord
- rotary tool (Dremel) with multipurpose cutting attachment
- fluid acrylics
- acrylic ink
- paintbrushes
- sanding block
- acrylic paint markers (DecoArt)
- glue
- small wood blocks

1 In this example, I am working on a piece of deep-cradled Claybord and laying out smaller pieces that were cut from a flat piece. Use these small dimensional parts to plan out your composition—where you are going to want the cutout holes vs. where you want the raised parts. Make a quick sketch directly onto the board.

2 Cut shapes in the deep-cradled board using a multipurpose cutting tool.

3 When using analogous colors, I tend to gather all the variations I have on hand and use them together to build interest in the layers. I previously did a little carving on this board, which you may or may not want. Then paint with fluid acrylics and acrylic ink, allowing under-layers to show through.

4 The round cutout shape was a little too round for me, so I roughed up the edges to make it more organic. After you have sanded your small parts, start to paint them with fluid acrylics. Add detail and trim work with the acrylic markers.

Got Power?

If you own power tools, drill a hole into the clayboard and then cut your window areas using a jigsaw or a scroll saw (if you want to make more intricate cuts). The scroll saw also works well on the flat clayboard pieces for cutting shapes that may be used in your art. I like to precut shapes and have a variety of them on hand to choose from. Of course, you don't even need to use clayboard for the shapes; any other material would work, too. I simply like claybaord because it offers the carving option in addition to its other versatile characteristics.

5 Don't forget to paint any edges that will be visible. I also paint any wood blocks or scraps that will be used "behind the scenes"—black is the best choice so they won't be noticed.

6 First glue down the pieces that are going to be right against your base clayboard. Then glue the blocks that will hold the raised parts. Then place your final raised parts. The front side is done. Allow to dry before proceeding.

7 Glue shapes behind the window.

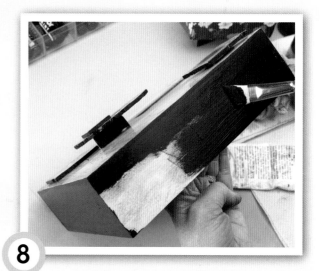

8 Finally, if you like, paint the sides of the cradled board. The sides could also be a continuation of your art, or they could be left bare.

What's in Your Pantry?

I love all these small painted parts so much that I have a hankering to go sculptural with them. I imagine painting all shapes and sizes and assembling them in some abstract (of course!) fashion so they stand on their own. If you find yourself accumulating lots of small shapes and pieces, why not try making a mobile (à la Alexander Calder)?

This large diptych includes many of the same techniques that the previous project did. More "windows" add more dimension and the opportunity for additional levels. When displayed with proper lighting, shadow play creates even more complexity.

FLAVORS

When I think of flavor—and I'm talking about swoon-producing flavor—words like *luscious* or *succulent* come to mind. I recall the first time I had molten chocolate cake many, many years ago before it became mainstream (and a dietary staple); a perfectly poached egg on top of organic baby spinach; lemon curd on a delicate, flaky scone. But alas . . . I'm not here to talk about food at the moment.

I am talking about flavor as in style or mood or voice. For instance, Claudine Hellmuth's work is widely recognized in mixed-media circles; she has established a look (or flavor) that is instantly known. My "Common Denominator" series has a flavor. Our guest artists Deb Trotter and Heather Haymart also have a flavor, as do many of the other artists featured in this book. Flavor, as I'm using the word, relates to voice. It can be difficult to find your artist voice, and the best advice I could give is to make lots and lots of art, all the time, every day. Then one day you will look up and realize you have a voice that is all your own.

To start our flavor exploration, we will limit our work to rigid substrates. I will offer up some very diverse techniques that will hopefully send you into tasty explorations of your own.

If life were predictable it would cease to be life, and be without flavor.
—Eleanor Roosevelt

Guest Artist:
Heather Haymart

Heather Haymart grew up surrounded by women making art, be it ceramics, crochet, paintings or drawings. As a child, she had a habit of using every card that came in the mail as a reference for creating new drawings. It surprised no one when she went to college for art, receiving a B.S. in education in addition to her B.F.A.

Today she is a generous and giving teacher of private lessons and group classes for children and adults, in addition to doing art fairs. She also exhibits at three different galleries in the greater St. Louis area—two at which she partners. She is blunt when she admits, "I am living my dream."

But it wasn't always that way. After college, she went on to teach middle and high school for six years and, oddly, that was the least creative time of her life because she found herself "artistically tapped out by the end of the day." Her summers were often filled with creating fiber sculptures. She decided to be a mural painter and did that for about two years. She stopped after she realized she didn't enjoy painting on location and when she could never get over the frustration of being asked, "Will this cost less if I take out the tree?"

When asked about creative blocks, Heather said she definitely has them because life is full of interruptions. She tries to use the interruptions to her advantage as a chance to clear her head, but if all else fails, she just muscles through. She feels that her daily sketchbook habit helps her because that is when she draws simply for pleasure. She finds art is healing but also fun and challenging; she makes art to stay sane.

Heather loves to cook and eat good food. She follows recipes but also finds herself improvising a lot. She recognizes that her process with art and food is similar. She adores simplicity. Her favorite meal is a bottle of red wine, good bread, smoked Gouda and olive oil with fresh ground pepper, ideally served right on the cutting boards. Yum!

Recipe for: *Heather's Favorite Pasta*

- a few fresh basil leaves, cut a chiffonade
- a few summer tomatoes, diced
- penne pasta
- a couple cloves of fresh garlic
- handful of freshly grated Parmesan cheese
- olive oil

→ Sauté the garlic in olive oil while boiling the pasta. Drain pasta; add garlic and olive oil and all the remaining ingredients. Toss to mix. Serve with bread and red wine.

Icing Panels

One of my favorite things to bake is plain ol' sugar cookies, the kind where you use cookie cutters. I make hearts and stars in various sizes, then bask in icing them with coordinating colors—there is nothing more appealing than a plate full of beautifully iced cookies. Yum!

Wood Icing is just as fun. This is a product that Heather's mom, Rose, created to use in the decorative finishing industry—on walls and furniture to be specific. Heather started using it in fine-art applications and developed her own style of painting that is done completely with Wood Icing.

Using Heather's influence and her mom's product, we will work within a grid to create our own abstract panel painting.

Ingredients

- pencil
- pre-gessoed Masonite panels
- stencils
- Wood Icing Textura (or hard molding paste)
- Wood Icing Fissure (or crackle medium)
- palette knife
- tools/items to create texture
- acrylic paints
- paintbrushes
- sanding block
- collage material (optional)
- acrylic paint marker (DecoArt)

Grid Work

For me, approaching a grid is comforting. I know that might sound weird when speaking about an abstract painting, but seriously, I like boxes and compartments. A grid lends immediate organization to your piece. You can work each section separately; just remember to stay within your color palette. A little bit of subtle glazing with fluid acrylic or ink will help blend the areas together.

1

Sketch out a grid style composition and apply texture to a few areas using a stencil and Wood Icing Textura. Clean your stencil before the icing hardens on it.

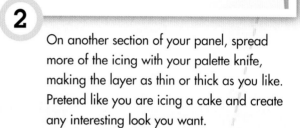

2

On another section of your panel, spread more of the icing with your palette knife, making the layer as thin or thick as you like. Pretend like you are icing a cake and create any interesting look you want.

3

Press a series of shapes into the icing. Here I am using various sizes of copper pipes to create graduated circles.

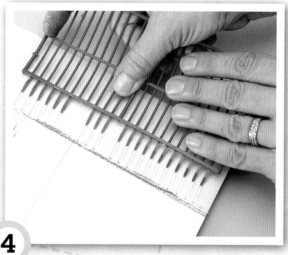

4

Spread icing over one more section of your panel, and this time, drag (comb) something through the medium, such as this section of miniature fencing I'm using here. You can also use any type of mark-making tool, a stick or whatever. You can even write into the Wood Icing using the tip of a pencil (dip it in water first).

For this project, I am using the complementary colors of red and green. Typically, these are holiday colors, yet they don't come off that way here. One reason is the variations in red, from the bright pop of the paint pen to the earthiness of Burnt Sienna. Also, the green I have chosen is not the typical green, but is a more modern version. Don't be afraid of complementary colors.

Complementary Colors

5

To create a really great crackle, apply Wood Icing Fissure to a section of your panel. You can apply this with a knife or with a brush.

6

Set your board aside to dry. When the textured areas are dry, sand them with a sanding block to smooth the sharp areas of the hardened icing.

7

For one grid section, consider adding a collage element using paper that you have printed yourself (see Collagraph Plate on page 60). Here I am using a section of a collagraph scrap.

8

Begin painting your board. Watch what happens when you paint over the areas with the Fissure (crackle medium). Painting one color and then dry brushing with another is a good way to create depth in your piece.

9

Complete the piece with other elements, such as game pieces, buttons, ephemera, etc., and add final depth with a bit of black to outline the individual areas. An acrylic paint marker can bring back a punch of color.

What's in Your Pantry?

Because Wood Icing was originally made for decorative purposes, why not scrounge flea markets for a piece of furniture to use this product on? I mean, admit it, you're already hanging around flea markets (I know I am). And knowing about Wood Icing has transformed my shopping experience. Now I can see potential in just about anything! See, Wood Icing is tough! With the consistency of peanut butter, it has the ability to revamp even the most damaged item, but it's incredibly sturdy, too.

Both of these pieces were created using a grid composition. You can see how repeated use of circles (in varying sizes) strengthens the composition.

Guest Artist: Deb Trotter

Although you may think of her as a "yee-ha" kinda cowgirl, Deb Trotter is really just a romantic at heart. Her work harkens back to the good ol' days when cowboys sat around a campfire cooking a can of beans as their horses stood tied up nearby.

Growing up in the south, Deb loved all things western and longed to live in the West. Moving to Cody, Wyoming, as an adult was simply a dream come true. She had previously done decorative painting and took her first collage class in 2003 with Claudine Hellmuth. She said, "I felt like *this* was what I was supposed to do." Her self-education continued with drawing and painting classes and then lots of self-taught Photoshop—all of which is uses in the work she makes today.

Deb has transformed herself into the sassy goddess of all things Western, with her humorous observations making their way onto a line of greeting cards and her images being featured on leather goods for Icon Shoes. Deb also has collaborated on a line of handbags. Her tagline "Cowboy's Sweetheart: Joyous Art, Cowgirl Attitude" really sums it up.

Although she does love food, Deb concedes that she isn't huge on cooking unless she can do it on the grill, and that *must* be over charcoal or wood. Don't even think about using a gas grill. She is, however, adept at the old-time recipes passed down through her family; it's only the newer ones that elude her, something she jokes could be either an altitude issue or an inconsistent oven. Deb's husband tells her she is stuck in a time warp. And you know what? I think that's a good thing.

© Deb Trotter

5   6   7   8   9   10

Taste of Klimt

Deb Trotter's work is
so stylized it makes me think of
another favorite artist—Gustav
Klimt. He definitely had his own
flavor. His highly ornamental
paintings explored a range of
emotional subjects.

Starting out as a decorative
painter and muralist, Klimt's work
was lush with gold and silver and
organic shape. I think Klimt would
adore the idea that his work
inspired me to do this "high-fash-
ion" project.

We will play on clayboard,
using gold foil as a background.
Just as Deb and Klimt work their
detailed backgrounds, we will
also create patterns—some that
emulate doodles and others that
require a palette knife. In the
process we will "Klimt up" a
fashion model and create a retro-
inspired piece.

Ingredients

- clayboard substrate, anysize or type
- gold foil
- tacking iron
- picture from a fashion magazine
- black glaze pen
- palette knife
- acrylic paints (Claudine Hellmuth Studio)
- acrylic paint markers (DecoArt)
- paintbrushes
- collage elements, such as punched paper elements (optional)
- gel medium (optional)
- awl or other scratching tool

1 Position gold foil over the clayboard and use a tacking iron to adhere the foil randomly to different sections of the board.

2 Cut out the shape of a figure from a magazine or newspaper, and use a pen to trace around the figure onto the board.

3 Add simple lines to complete the picture and to sketch out the background and horizon line. I have divided the clayboard into three basic sections.

4 Use the palette knife to apply heavy-bodied acrylics to one section of the background. I typically work with two or three analogous colors and use the point of the knife to work the paint around my drawing. Sometimes I will blend the colors with the knife, and other times I scrape some of the paint away to reveal the gold areas. I work in little strokes to create a consistent look that will appear almost pattern-like.

Your Voice

It isn't easy to develop your own voice, and I have a ton of admiration for folks who find their voice and stick with it. Sometimes I get hypercritical of my own efforts, especially when I start to explore new ideas and get side-railed. I sometimes feel like I have lost my voice, but I have found that eventually it will come back.

5 For another section of the background, I make long stripes of color by pulling the knife through the paint. Once again, I cover the gold but also allow it to peek out in certain areas.

6 For the last section, the one below the horizon line, try doodling with paint pens to create a series of geometric shapes. Here I am using three colors to make assorted squares and rectangles. Don't forget to leave some shapes gold.

7 After completing the geometric shapes, you can fine-tune things with a black pen and add in a few more details. Black and white really helps the color pop.

8 One way to add interest is with shapes cut out from decorative punches. I'm applying these little flowers with a bit of gel medium.

9 For the dress, I have added paint over the top of the entire area, then wiped the paint away to reveal the gold. I don't want to do too much in this area, choosing to leave her as more of a golden silhouette.

10 Using a black glaze pen, add further details to both the figure and the background as you see fit.

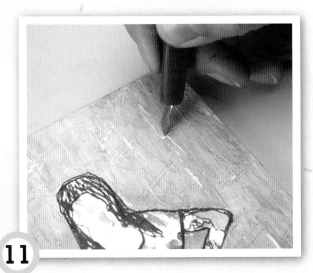

11 Texture can be added by carving out some lines with an awl or other scratching tool, such as the cross-hatching marks I've made here. By carving into the clayboard, some of the white background pops back.

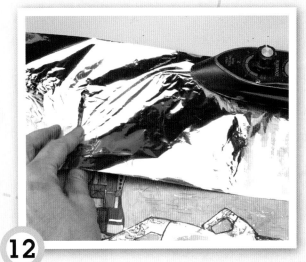

12 Finally, add some foil back in just around the edges using a tacking iron.

What's in Your Pantry?

Consider painting your substrate black before starting, or work on black scratch board. Trace your subject onto the black surface and allow that area to remain black, as a silhouette. Proceed with the gold foil in other areas. Use several light colors, including white, as you use the palette knife on the background to create some contrast. Working in a very limited palette will make this piece especially exciting.

These three pieces were done following the steps outlined. I used some variety in my doodling to instill a different mood in each.

Guest Artist:
Claudine Hellmuth

The wonder girl of the mixed-media world, Claudine Hellmuth, is truly one of my art superheroes. She does it all, from painting to drawing to product design. She's taught, written books, done gallery shows, licensed products and successfully crossed over into other arenas. But I'm getting ahead of myself.

I first met Claudine in 2002 when I took a series of classes from her. I was just a budding collage artist, and she was, well, just a baby—still so young, yet wildly talented; a generous teacher who inspired me in many ways. Teaching workshops was not her initial plan. After college, she worked as a web designer but was getting publicity for her vintage collages. After many requests, she started to teach some workshops on the side, thinking it might be a stepping-stone to her goal of having her own business. Three books later, she has long lost the day job, is still teaching and has successfully expanded into other directions, including the line of Ranger products recently added to the mix.

Many people were surprised and even shocked when Claudine abandoned her signature vintage look and introduced her Poppet line. At a time that appeared to be the pinnacle of her career, she completely shifted gears to a more whimsical retro look—work that had a decided graphic design influence. What some of her fans may not know is that behind the scenes, Claudine was burned out. She had been making the vintage works since her college days, after all, and had mentally become bored with them. She had strong feelings about the move, saying, "I wanted to do more drawing and bring my hands back into the work." After a dry spell of false starts and self-labeled "bad art," the Poppets were born.

Not one to rest on her laurels, Claudine has had great success with the Poppets, even making them with Martha Stewart on her show. They remain quite popular as custom pieces.

Claudine is the exception to my thinking about artists and food. When asked about her interest in cooking, Claudine laughed as she tried to explain. "My husband learned to cook because I think he realized (that if left up to me) we would be eating cereal and popcorn all our lives." A vegetarian, Claudine confesses to being a picky eater. "I have the palate of a four-year-old child." Obviously, her *paint* palette is much more expansive.

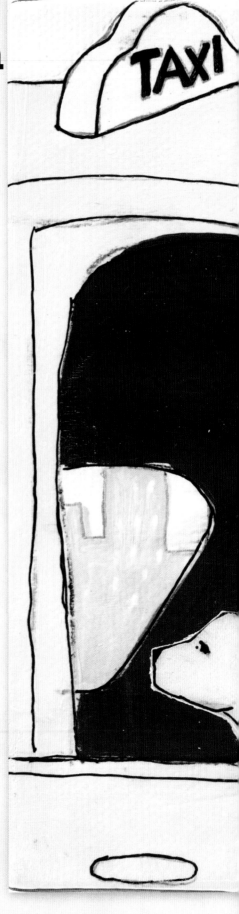

Collage Painting

I made my very first collage when I was four years old. My mom saved it and gave it to me several years ago. I made my second collage for a study group assignment in 2000. The group was called The Artist's Way, obviously based on Julia Cameron's book of the same title. Having been in corporate America for so many years, I was living under a rock and had never heard of the book. I signed up for the class by accident because of miscommunication with a friend of mine. Incredibly, I thought I was signing up for some sort of weekly arts-and-crafts session. My friend quit after two weeks, but I persisted and even signed up for the following session to study *Vein of Gold*.

My love for collage led me to study with a variety of teachers, including Claudine. In 2001, I developed my "Common Denominator" series, so named because I used unidentified pictures that I found at flea markets and estate sales. I chose people from all walks of life and made up new stories about them. I came to believe it was my unspoken mission to celebrate the fact that people are more alike than different. To this day, I love making vintage collages. Come join me!

Ingredients

→ collage items, two- and three-dimensional
→ MDF panel
→ gel medium
→ paintbrush
→ acrylic paints
→ stamp pad

1 Start by collaging some background pieces onto the panel using gel medium both under and over the paper.

2 With a couple of background pieces down, I start piecing additional elements together almost like a puzzle. Gather elements that you like and think about how they can work together. Move them around and try out a variety of compositions.

3 Put a thin coat of Titanium Buff and Titanium White over the collage, as necessary, to blend the background.

4 Add color as you see fit, keeping much of it sheer so you can still see your collage papers.

Personal Symbols

It is important for me to create meaning within my pieces. Although it may appear that my collage elements are quite "random," they have actually been selected with care. In this piece, for instance, there are several elements that are part of my personal symbolism. As you make more and more work, notice items that recur in your pieces and see if you can discover what they might mean to you. Development of your own symbolic language will add strength and significance to your work.

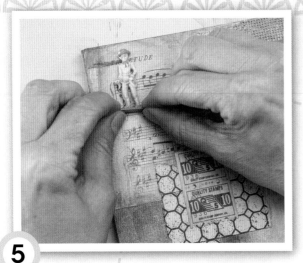

5

After some color is down, I often add more collage papers over the top, which will keep their original color. Dimensional objects can be added using gel medium or tacky glue, depending on the weight of the objects. Here I have added a piece of an old screen door using gel medium and a little plastic cowboy using tacky glue.

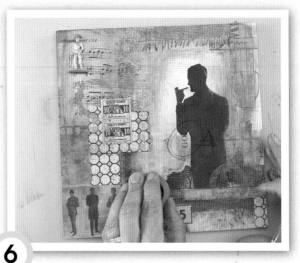

6

Stamping imagery is a good way to tie the whole piece together. I enjoy stamps that imply texture or perhaps a random geometric shape. Rather than using a stamp pad, I paint acrylic on the stamp so it blends with my painting.

7

I like to add some shadowing using a stamp pad. I often outline portions of the collage papers by rubbing the pad along their edges.

What's in Your Pantry?

Use fabric; make your subjects three-dimensional; incorporate moving parts. Draw around your central image; paint out the background; paint in a new background; paint different clothing on your subject. There are so many variations on the theme of collage that the sky is the limit. I think it is interesting to use the same picture but put the person into different backgrounds and create new personas. Another fun thing, instead of using just the photo, cut around the subject and use the background. You may want to use both the background and the photo or just the background, allowing the edges to simply suggest the subject matter.

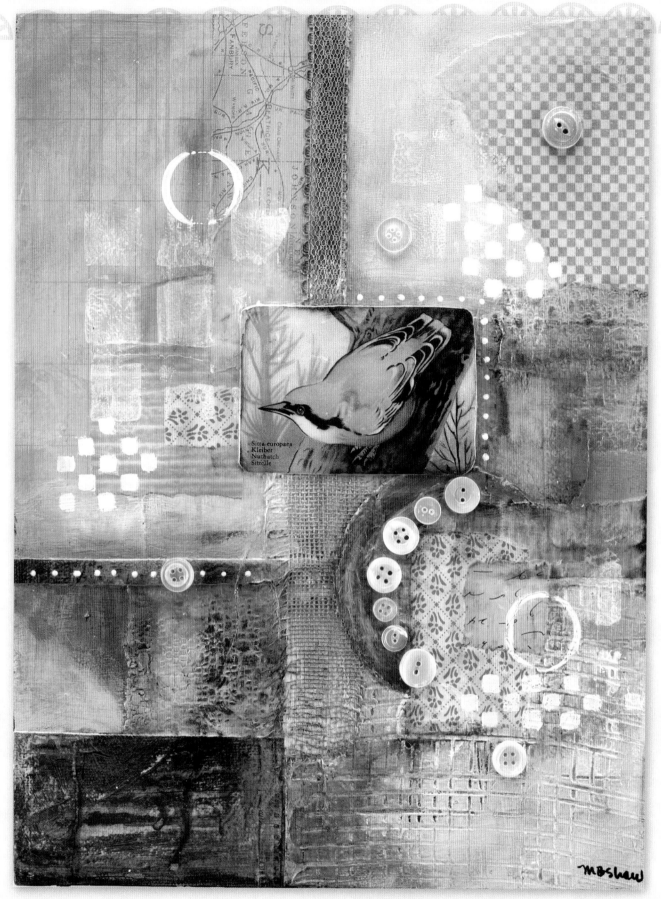

If you examine this piece as well as the one on the previous page, you will see they are done on somewhat of a grid composition too. Texture was added to this piece using carving as well as with the addition of buttons and scraps of fabric.

COMBINATIONS

When I think of "combinations," I think of food such as cassoulet and paella, two of my absolute favorites. I think I like them so much because their recipes are loose and free. You basically work with whatever you have on hand, which I adore. And yeah, making art is exactly the same!

So what happens when you take all the stuff you know and put it together? You create tasty combinations: lots of layers and textures and colors—all good! That's what the artists in this section do—push it to the max, sometimes using unexpected supplies or perhaps mixing things up in ways that deviate from the norm. This often results in the creation of a flavor that is all their own.

It can sometimes require a critical eye to pull off a lot of different techniques in the same piece, and that is where your inner editor needs to jump in. In this chapter, we will see works by Katie Kendrick, John Hammons and Judy Wise. We will use this inspiration to create some inventive pieces of our own, making good use of primarily discarded materials.

A good head **and a good heart are always a formidable combination.**
—Nelson Mandela

Guest Artist:
Katie Kendrick

Coming from a musical family, Katie Kendrick grew up singing and playing both the viola and piano. Everyone assumed she would pursue a musical path; that was her family's "thing." Yet she pined for visual art, too shy to make her desires known. Years later, while on a quest of spiritual inquiry, her interest in visual arts resurfaced, and this time she knew she couldn't walk away.

Known for her soul-inspired and thought-provoking work, Katie has explored every angle of the mixed-media world, from pottery to fabric to collage, painting and sculpture. Although she has been a very popular workshop teacher, she is ready for some time off so she can regroup and allow somebody else "with more juice" to take over. She looks forward to using this time to explore and allow her art to take her wherever it wants to go.

After high school, Katie spent time hitchhiking around the country. She is a true "seeker" in every sense of the word and says that the path of inquiry is the single most important thing to her and fully guides her art. Whether teaching or exhibiting, she hopes to inspire people to connect with the dynamic flow of the universe.

A lover of good food, Katie and her husband have always maintained a garden, although they are in a rebuilding stage due to a recent flood on their property. She seeks to cook and eat the freshest and best ingredients she can find, preferably something she grows herself or from local and sustainable sources. As with many artists, it is the sensual quality of food that appeals to her, and she would prefer to make do with less in order to buy the quality of food she demands.

When her kids were growing up, she cooked frequently, often using unusual items (for that time) such as tempeh and soy milk. She tried to grow as much as she could herself. Although temporarily derailed from gardening, she is in the process of designing a terraced garden that will allow her and her husband to garden while standing up, an influence she learned from the Chinese. She also wants a new chicken house.

Katie's Indian Coconut Lentil Soup

Recipe for:

(Use organic items whenever possible.)

- 1 lb. lentils, rinsed
- 2½ quarts water
- 1½ T. curry powder
- 2½ T. turmeric
- 4 tsp. coriander
- ½ tsp. freshly ground black pepper
- pinch cloves
- pinch cinnamon
- 1 cup chopped celery
- 2 large carrots, sliced in rounds or diced
- 1½ T. Celtic sea salt (or other good salt)
- 2 large fresh tomatoes or 1 15-oz. can chopped tomatoes
- 2 13.5-oz. cans coconut milk
- 3 T. coconut oil
- pinch cayenne pepper
- 1 onion, finely chopped
- 3 cloves garlic

→ Bring the first 12 ingredients to boil in a soup pot, then cover and cook on low for 45 minutes, then add the coconut milk.

→ Pour coconut oil into a separate pan. Add the remaining ingredients and sauté until golden brown.

→ Add the sautéed mixture to the soup pot, simmer another 5 to 10 minutes.
Makes 3+ quarts.

They gather in heedless beauty.

Cardboard Collage

My name is Mary Beth Shaw, and I am a pack rat. I save all sorts of things because I can see potential in nearly every scrap or recycled item I touch. I swear it is a curse to be like this. Over the years, I have accumulated countless bins of things that I just know I will want to use one day. Take my discarded painted paper towels: I started saving these years ago and have an enormous collection. They can be sewn together to create funky wrapping paper; they can be used in collage; they make pretty packing supplies . . .

This Cardboard Collage was inspired by Katie Kendrick. She does amazing things to cardboard, transforming it in such stunning ways that I can't even figure out how she achieves such beauty. So let's play a little bit and see what we can make.

Ingredients

- scrap corrugated cardboard
- collage elements
- gel medium
- paintbrush
- sanding block
- acrylic paints
- stencil
- craft knife
- fabric
- screening materials
- pencil

1

Start with a scrap of ordinary cardboard. Collage assorted elements onto the surface of the board using gel medium. Use a sanding block to remove excess paper from the edges.

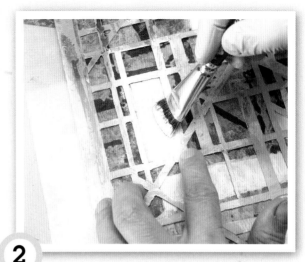

2

Paint out certain geometric areas using a stencil. I am using the same stencil that has been printed on the tissue. The use of similar patterns will make the work cohesive.

3

Use a craft knife to gently cut away the top layer of paper on the cardboard and then roll the paper back to reveal the corrugation of underneath.

Art Repurposed

Think of different ways you can repurpose supplies, scraps or other products you have on hand. For instance, I scanned my hand-cut stencil and then made the inverse image, which I printed on light brown tissue paper. The screen used in this project came off a screen door we replaced in our house. I find that its distressed condition is perfect for my use. And the cardboard itself is used packaging material.

4 Fabric can be glued to areas of the board or the inside of the peeled-back flaps. You could also insert a little message here.

5 I scrape away the fuzzy paper parts along each cardboard ridge and then paint shadows along the sides.

6 To complete, I glue down the screening material, using gel medium, and I go back for touch-up detail with a pencil.

What's in Your Pantry?

Use any size of scrap corrugated cardboard to create little cardboard windows such as the ones we cut in this project. Keep them on hand for use in future pieces so you can easily grab one when you need it. You can paint them, distress them with ink or sandpaper, or simply leave them plain. I enjoy putting a word in these windows. When I am sorting through vintage papers, such as old book pages, I paint over all except my favorite words, using white paint. The contrast of the paint with the yellowed paper makes my chosen words really pop out. I glue them onto the cardboard windows in such a way that the flaps fold back to reveal the cryptic words.

These pieces incorporate scrap bits of cardboard. The three-dimensional quality of these scraps adds a funky twist to these paintings.

Photos by Greg Barth

Guest Artist:
John Hammons

John Hammons is talented in so many areas. He is like the kid in school who you want to hate except for the fact that you like him too much. Practically an art savant, I have sat beside John in class watching as he easily masters a complex technique while I am still struggling with some basic concept. He's brilliant like that, and I have come to expect this from a guy who is a physician in his day job and simply uses art as his "outlet and escape."

Adept at many mediums from drawing and painting to calligraphy to fiber, quilting and macramé, John has been making art since his childhood. His interest was supported by his mother, and he remembers "the year I got an art set from Sears for Christmas. It had so many different mediums and was in a shiny red case." This led to painting lessons; he still has an oil painting he did during that time.

With so many interests, including gardening, cooking and decorating (in addition to art), John is still trying to find the medium that fits him best. He doesn't aspire to exhibit his work or even create an entire body of work, but enjoys his current exploration of the human face and portraiture. For the last few years, he has been drawn to the human face and letterforms, and loves looking at art that combines these two things. Recent trips to Italy have fueled this love. He admires the work of Duccio, Frida Kahlo, Mexican Santos and the portraits of Misty Mawn.

An excellent cook, John worked at a kitchen store several years ago during a leave of absence from medicine. He was exposed to local chefs and their classes on a daily basis, and this allowed him to be more creative in his own cooking. He is definitely a foodie and seeks to prepare the highest quality food. He feels that with cooking, like art, you need to be comfortable in the medium before improvisation is possible. He says, "When I put the hours in practicing techniques that I have learned in classes, then I find that the work starts to take on my own voice."

See? I told you he was brilliant.

FRIDA
determined life
crippled · crushed
broken
emotion poured on
canvas
ARTIST

Abstract Letter Forms

I use text in my work all the time. Perhaps this harkens back to my journalism roots. I just delight in hiding little word messages in my art. Sometimes my letters and words are super-obvious—a caption of sorts—but sometimes they are hidden and intentionally puzzling.

This project, based on the calligraphy in John's piece, uses oversized letters in an abstract way. Some people might not even realize they are letters, or that there is a hidden meaning—or is there?

Ingredients

- substrate (I used Masonite)
- gesso
- sandpaper
- drywall tape
- acrylic paints
- paintbrushes
- pencil
- gel medium
- black pen that will write over acrylic, such as Uniball Vision (waterproof)
- letters for embellishment

1 Gesso the Masonite and allow to dry. Sand lightly, then gesso again. Sand once more until substrate is smooth.

2 Tape drywall tape over the surface and then dab paint on top. I used Titanium Buff paint. Remove the tape and allow the painted/textured surface to dry before proceeding.

3 Using a pencil, make an appealing layout using very large letters. Trace around them to define your composition.

4 Paint each section as desired. Using gel medium, glue some of the drywall tape over selected letters. Doodle or make random marks in certain areas.

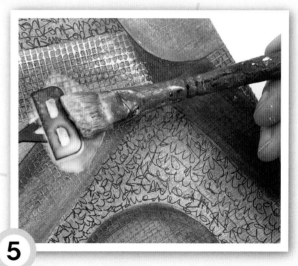

5 Add additional letters for embellishment, then glue down. Continue adding layers of paint until your desired look is achieved.

What's in Your Pantry?

Throughout this book, we have used a lot of color, yet neutral artwork can be so beautiful. Think white on white with perhaps some faded yellow, buff or linen. When I use vintage book pages in my work, I always tear the edges off each sheet right up to the print. This leaves a strip of torn paper that is plain with no words written on it. Rather than tossing these strips in the trash, I keep them all in a box. Even though they are approximately the same color, there is such variation of hue. You can use these bits of paper to make a collage. Organize the strips a la mosaic style or glue them down in a more random fashion. All the faded and yellowed pieces will make a striking piece, whether used on their own or as part of another artwork.

When making art with abstract letter forms, I some-times allow part of the letter to extend beyond the edge of the susbrate.

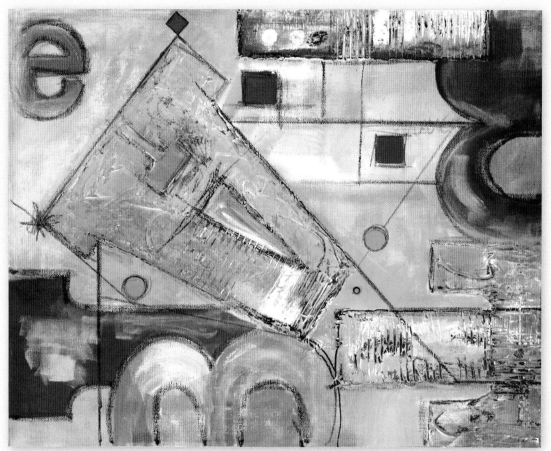

Photos by Greg Barth

When painting these pieces, I don't necessarily follow the composition set by the letters. For instance, here I painted some of the letters into the background so the viewer needs to search for them to see them.

Guest Artist:
Judy Wise

Judy Wise spent many years as an "art fair artist" before she discovered the mixed-media world. She has worked her way through a bunch of different mediums, from leather to jewelry, to batik, pen-and-ink, etching, watercolor and painting on the reverse side of acrylic. One day, she was with a group of art fair people and heard about Art & Soul in Portland. She immediately signed up for a bookmaking class. And, once she attended, she knew she had something to offer. It was then that she ended what she refers to as "years of isolation." She loves the camaraderie of the workshops—meeting other teachers and students.

Earning a minor in art during college, Judy has "taken a million classes since then" and is especially influenced by Japanese-inspired things. Her art fairs have tapered off in recent years, but she still does a few of her favorites now and then.

When queried about her favorite media, she hesitates for a second and then replies honestly, "Whatever my hand touches first is the thing I love the most." At this moment, she is into gluing stuff down and messing with it. She finds any artistic activity to be "grist for the mill" because there is just so much information at our fingertips; she can never do too much exploring.

The most interesting things for Judy involves a process of resistance and challenge. She loves to mess around with supplies and play. Currently writing a book that focuses on plaster with Stephanie Lee, she describes plaster as "the poor man's ceramic" and loves the discoveries they have made regarding this "unusual and amazing medium."

Judy adores food and is lucky to have a world-class gardener in the family—her husband, John. He grows all sorts of organic produce, including a special type of heirloom tomato he developed from seed. Rather than choosing complex recipes, Judy always turns to fresh and local ingredients and dubs "anything that includes garlic and olive oil" her specialty, saying she could easily live in Spain. She enjoys making bruschetta but is quick to specify that it must be wood-fired.

Recipe for: *Judy's Favorite Summer Meal*

→ Go out into the garden around 4 p.m. when the sun is high and the tomatoes are fragrant and warm. Round up the usual suspects. Grab a couple of lemon cucumbers while you're at it and a nice red onion. Make thin slices of everything in the kitchen and add salt, pepper and a squeeze of lemon juice or a pour of rice vinegar. Serve with a tall glass of cold well water and sit down to what has become my favorite summer meal.

Abstract With Discarded Material

Dig deeper and pull out some stuff from your garbage. I grabbed a security envelope and a scrap of tissue paper that I had tossed, plus some bits of foil that were laying on my table. I have this idea I want to show you: a landscape of sorts, with terraced layers.

Ingredients

- → substrate (I used clayboard)
- → discarded items for collage
- → acrylic gel medium
- → paintbrushes
- → sanding block
- → acrylic ink
- → spray bottle with water
- → tissue paper
- → acrylic paints
- → alcohol ink

1

Start with a scrap of ordinary cardboard. Collage assorted elements onto the surface of the board using gel medium. Use a sanding block to remove excess paper from the edges.

2

A transparent glaze of ink will help tie these elements together. Add more ink and spritz with water, allowing some to run. Then let dry. Use a sanding block to remove excess paper from the edges.

3

Tear several lengths of tissue paper into strips that are 1" to 2" (3cm to 5cm) wide and roll them with some soft gel medium.

Be Transparent

Tissue must certainly be the most versatile paper around. I have always adored its transparent quality, but lately I am using it more and more. For instance, you can easily build texture by gluing it flat and then pushing it into interesting wrinkle shapes (while the glue is still wet). You can write on small pieces, then collage your pieces. If you gently sand the edges while it is still wet, the tissue will easily integrate into your background. You can also build shapes with it and create more three-dimensional elements on your pieces, because it is quite strong once it has been coated with medium.

4

While the rolls are still wet, shape however you like and press them gently onto the painting. Apply additional medium over the top to seal them.

5

Paint the piece as you see fit. To tint the envelope window, I applied some alcohol ink to it and spritzed it with plain alcohol.

6

I placed my photo behind the window element and glued it down with gel medium. Here I've also added some tiny Styrofoam balls that I found on the floor; I thought they looked like eggs, and my circle appeared as the perfect little nest.

What's in Your Pantry?

I keep a bin in my studio of leftover parts. Every time I am finished with a collage, I dump all my scraps into the bin. Sometimes when I start a new piece, I don't even pull out new material but just work completely with scraps. There is something so appealing about collections of miscellaneous pieces. Enjoy the challenge of putting them together in a meaningful manner.

Starting with unstretched canvas, I assembled a lot of discarded materials and used my sewing machine to make this piece. I enjoy the raw edges and unrefined borders that resulted.

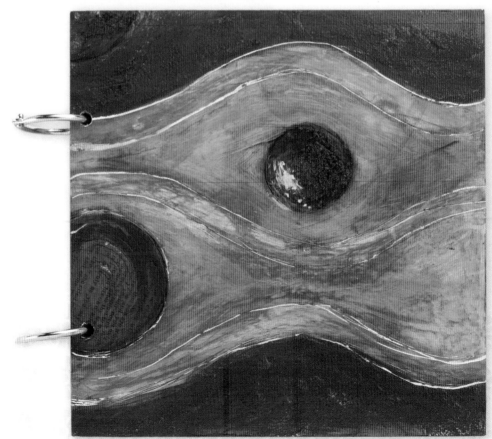

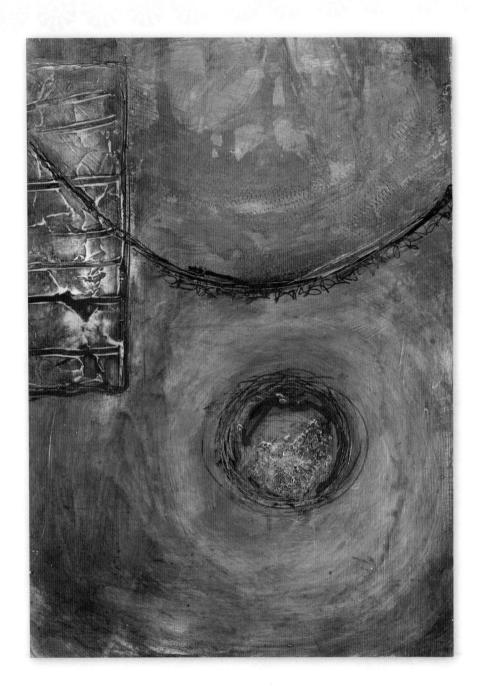
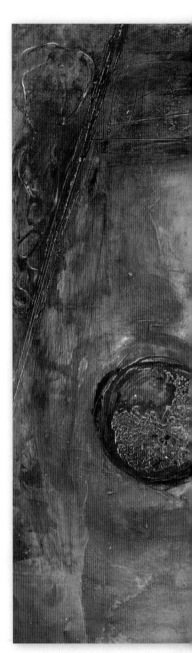

Guest Artists

Sarah Ahearn Bellemare
www.sarahearn.com
www.sarahearn.blogspot.com

Shari Beaubien
www.sharibeaubien.com
www.sharibeaubien.typepad.com

Tonia Davenport
www.toniadavenport.typepad.com

Dolan Geiman
www.dolangeiman.com
www.dolangeiman.blogspot.com
www.dolangeiman.etsy.com
info@dolangeiman.com

John Hammons
www.johnhammons.blogspot.com
johnhammons@charter.net

Heather Haymart
www.heatherhaymart.com
www.heatherhaymart.blogspot.com

Claudine Hellmuth
www.collageartist.com
www.claudinehellmuth.blogspot.com

Katie Kendrick
www.katiekendrick.com
www.joyouslybecoming.typepad.com
joyouslybecoming@q.com

Laura Lein-Svencner
www.lauralein-svencner.com
lonecrow4@comcast.net

Elizabeth MacCrellish
www.squamartworkshops.com
elizabeth@squamartworkshops.com

Misty Mawn
www.mistymawn.typepad.com
mistymawn@gmail.com

Julie Snidle
jasnidle@aol.com

Deb Trotter
www.debtrotter.com
www.cowboyssweetheart.typepad.com
debtrotter1@gmail.com

Susan Tuttle
www.ilkasattic.com
www.ilkasattic.blogspot.com

Judy Wise
www.judywise.com
www.judywise.blogspot.com
judywise@canby.com

Resources

Ampersand Art Supply

www.ampersandart.com

Claybord substrates

Aves Studio

www.avesstudio.com

Apoxie Sculpt clay

Golden Artist Colors, Inc.

www.goldenpaints.com

acrylic paints and mediums

Greg Barth

www.gregbarth.com

portfolio photography

Marvy Uchida

www.marvy.com

acrylic paint markers

PanPastel

www.panpastel.com

low-dust pastels

Ranger Industries

www.rangerink.com

Claudine Hellmuth Studio acrylic paints

Sennelier

www.sennelier.com

soft pastels, oil pastels

Sharpie

www.sharpie.com

Mean Streak permanent markers

Stencil Girl Products

www.stencilgirlproducts.blogspot.com

stencils, Wood Icing, rubber stamps

Unison Pastels

www.unisoncolour.co.uk

soft pastels

Wood Icing

www.woodicing.com

texture and crackle pastes

INDEX

abstract painting, 30–33, 83

alcohol inks, 31, 67-68, 118

aluminum foil, 69

Apoxie clay, 51–52, 55

Beaubien, Shari, 36–37

Bellemare, Sarah Ahearn, 22–23

black, 26, 63, 91

book, 38–41

Candle Shade, 48–55

canvas board, 8, 52

cardboard 68–69, 105–6,

cheese grater, 17

clayboard, 8, 16–17, 39, 41, 67, 75–76, 89

collage, 10, 14, 46, 60, 96–99, 104–6

collagraph 60–63

colors, 9, 13–33

    analogous, 75

    complementary, 83

    layering, 40

    primary, 24

    color theory, 24–27

    combinations, 101–19

crackle medium, 84

Davenport, Tonia, 64–65

deli paper, 63, 69

dental tools, 17

depth, 20, 50, 77

dimension, 41, 74, 77

diptych, 38

discarded materials, 116–19

fiber paste, 39

flavors, 79–99

gallery, 120–23

Geiman, Dolan, 72–73

gesso, 18, 45

Glass Bead Gel, 40

glazing, 83

glue, 10

grids, 83

Hammons, John, 108–9

Haymart, Heather, 80–81

Hellmuth, Claudine, 94–95

Icing Panels, 82–85

implied texture, 44

inks, 9, 11, 30

Kendrick, Katie, 102–3

Klimt, Gustav, 88

layers/layering, 40, 41, 57–77

Lein-Svencner, Laura, 46–47

letter forms, 110–13

MacCrellish, Elizabeth, 28–29

Magic Eraser, 40

markers, acrylic, 9, 20

matte medium, 18, 20

Mawn, Misty, 14–15

mobile, 76

mosaic, 26

organization, 9

paints, 9, 24

    acrylic, 61

    making them run, 19

palette

    earthy, 26

    limited, 24, 32, 91

palette knife, 88

palette pages, 27

papers, 8, 69

    deli, 63, 69

    hand-painted, 60

    tissue, 117

    torn, 111

    transparent, 63

    vintage, 106

paper towels, 19

pastels, 9, 18, 20

personal symbols, 97

plastics, 70

plexiglass, 66–71

power tools, 75

primary colors, 24

printmaking, 60

repurposed materials, 105, 116–19

rotary tool, 10, 39

rubbings, 44, 45

sanding, 10, 49

scoring tool, 69

scraps, 118

shadows, 20, 77, 98

Snidle, Julie, 58–59

stencils, 50, 61

storage, 11

substrates, 8, 41

    black, 91

    prep work, 45

supplies, 8–11

symbols, personal, 97

Tar Gel, 40

text, 110–13

texture, 18, 20, 35–55, 68, 91, 99, 117

    implied, 44

    sampler, 44–45

tools, 10

transparency, 63, 117

triad colors 24–27

Trotter, Deb, 86–87

Tuttle, Susan, 42–43

value, 18, 40

voice, 79, 89

water-based products, 10

windows, 106

wire brushes, 17

Wise, Judy, 114–15

Wood Icing, 82–85

About
Mary Beth

Mary Beth Shaw is a mixed-media artist living in Wildwood, Missouri, with her husband and two cats. She teaches workshops nationally, participates in art fairs throughout the country and also exhibits in galleries. Although largely self-taught, Mary Beth has attended UC Berkeley Extension for art classes, in addition to a variety of workshops nationwide. She considers herself a seeker first and foremost.

Mary Beth believes that everyone has an inner artist who deserves the chance to come out and play. Her teaching style is energetic and fun; she thinks that mistakes can be our best lessons. She lives her life with passion and cherishes each and every moment.

Photo by Darryl Engeljohn

Author Contact:
Mary Beth Shaw
www.mbshaw.com
www.mbshaw.blogspot.com
www.stencilgirlproducts.blogspot.com

These are the best-ever, divine, to-die-for brownies. I got this recipe from a guy named Tim, who follows my blog. He was reading during a time when I was searching for the "perfect" brownie and sent me this recipe to try. I have modified it slightly and have to agree, it is pretty perfect! This makes an extremely fudgy-type brownie ('cause I see no reason to eat a cake-type brownie, but maybe that's just me!).

Best-Ever Brownies

Recipe for:

- 1 lb. semi-sweet chocolate chips (2¾ cups)
- 1 cup butter, cut into pieces
- ⅓ cup strong brewed coffee
- 4 large eggs, room temperature
- 1 cup sugar
- ½ cup flour
- 2 cups coarsely chopped walnuts or pecans, your pick
- 1 tsp. vanilla

↣ Preheat oven to 375°F (191°C).

↣ Melt butter, coffee and chocolate in a saucepan. Using a mixer, beat the eggs and sugar until light, add vanilla. Slowly incorporate the chocolate mixture into the egg mixture, adding a little at a time so you are careful to not cook the eggs. With a spoon, stir in flour and nuts.

↣ Line a 9" x 13" (23cm x 33cm) pan with foil and generously butter the foil. I put a double lining, running the foil one way, then the other way in the pan.

↣ Pour the batter into the pan. Bake 30 minutes or until just set around the edges. Cool on a wire rack. Cover and refrigerate overnight. They are best stored in the fridge.

Discover more inspiration with these North Light titles:

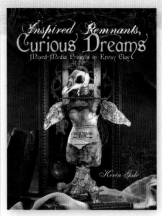

Digital Expressions

Susan Tuttle

Imagine flying through an inky night sky tethered to a red, heart-shaped balloon. Now imagine expressing that dream artistically. With Digital Expressions you can take ordinary photos and, with the help of Adobe Photoshop Elements, voice your flights of fancy.

Digital Expressions guides you through 25 digital art projects created with Adobe Photoshop Elements. With this easy-to-follow guide, you'll get inspired to tackle all kinds of digital mixed-media techniques using stock photography, custom brushes, textured backgrounds and your own digital photos.

ISBN-10: 1-60061-454-X
ISBN-13: 978-1-60061-454-5
paperback
144 pages
Z3940

Image Transfer Workshop

Darlene Olivia McElroy and Sandra Duran Wilson

Learn 35 transfer techniques (complete with finished art examples) that cover everything from basic tape and gel medium transfers to much more advanced techniques. McElroy's and Wilson's troubleshooting fixes will even enable you to work with your transfers that don't quite live up to expectations. *Image Transfer Workshop* provides a quick reference and examples of art using a variety of techniques that will inspire you to go beyond single transfer applications.

ISBN-10: 1-60061-160-5
ISBN-13: 978-1-60061-160-5
paperback
128 pages
Z2509

Encaustic Workshop

Patricia Seggebruch

Discover what happens when mixed media meets melted medium. In its purest form, encaustic painting is as simple as applying melted beeswax to an absorbent surface. In *Encaustic Workshop*, it becomes much more: a dynamic medium where anything goes and the possibilities are endless. Packed with step-by-step techniques, helpful tips and diverse examples of completed works, *Encaustic Workshop* brings all the accessibility and excitement of a mixed-media workshop to your own workspace. If you're a beginner, you'll find everything you need to know to get started. If you're a more advanced crafter or fine artist, you'll discover things you never knew you could do with encaustic.

ISBN-10: 1-60061-106-0
ISBN-13: 978-1-60061-106-3
paperback with flaps
128 pages
Z2089

Inspired Remnants, Curious Dreams

Kerin Gale

With the amazing properties of epoxy clay, your imagination is the only limit to the creative projects you'll indulge in, with a little bit of guidance from savvy sculptor, Kerin Gale. In *Inspired Remnants, Curious Dreams*, jewelry, accessories, décor and more are all explored and incorporate epoxy clay. You'll learn to add amazing textures and finishes to the clay, as well as use it to join objects together. Discover this addicting new medium today!

ISBN-10: 1-60061-944-4
ISBN-13: 978-1-60061-944-1
paperback
128 pages
Z6067

These and other fine F+W Media titles are available from your local craft retailer, bookstore, online supplier, or, visit our Web site at www.mycraftivitystore.com.